Data Science at the Command Line

D0731041

Jeroen Janssens

Beijing · Cambridge · Farnham · Köln · Sebastopol · Tokyo

Data Science at the Command Line

by Jeroen Janssens

Published by O'Reilly Media, Inc., 1005 Gravenstein Highway North, Sebastopol, CA 95472.

O'Reilly books may be purchased for educational, business, or sales promotional use. Online editions are also available for most titles (*http://safaribooksonline.com*). For more information, contact our corporate/institutional sales department: 800-998-9938 or *corporate@oreilly.com*.

Editors: Mike Loukides, Ann Spencer, and Marie Beaugureau	**Indexer:** Wendy Catalano
Production Editor: Matthew Hacker	**Interior Designer:** David Futato
Copyeditor: Kiel Van Horn	**Cover Designer:** Ellie Volckhausen
Proofreader: Jasmine Kwityn	**Illustrator:** Rebecca Demarest

October 2014:   First Edition

Revision History for the First Edition

2014-09-23:   First Release

See *http://oreilly.com/catalog/errata.csp?isbn=9781491947852* for release details.

978-1-491-94785-2

[LSI]

To my wife, Esther. Without her encouragement, support,
and patience, this book would surely have ended up in /dev/null.

Table of Contents

Preface

Data science is an exciting field to work in. It's also still very young. Unfortunately, many people, and especially companies, believe that you need new technology in order to tackle the problems posed by data science. However, as this book demonstrates, many things can be accomplished by using the command line instead, and sometimes in a much more efficient way.

Around five years ago, during my PhD program, I gradually switched from using Microsoft Windows to GNU/Linux. Because it was a bit scary at first, I started with having both operating systems installed next to each other (known as dual-boot). The urge to switch back and forth between the two faded and at some point I was even tinkering around with Arch Linux, which allows you to build up your own custom operating system from scratch. All you're given is the command line, and it's up to you what you want to make of it. Out of necessity I quickly became comfortable using the command line. Eventually, as spare time got more precious, I settled down with a GNU/Linux distribution known as Ubuntu because of its easy-of-use and large community. Nevertheless, the command line is still where I'm getting most of my work done.

It actually hasn't been too long ago that I realized that the command line is not just for installing software, system configuration, and searching files. I started learning about command-line tools such as cut, sort, and sed. These are examples of command-line tools that take data as input, do something to it, and print the result. Ubuntu comes with quite a few of them. Once I understood the potential of combining these small tools, I was hooked.

After my PhD, when I became a data scientist, I wanted to use this approach to do data science as much as possible. Thanks to a couple of new, open source command-line tools including scrape, jq, and json2csv, I was even able to use the command line for tasks such as scraping websites and processing lots of JSON data. In September 2013, I decided to write a blog post titled "Seven Command-Line Tools for Data Science." (*http://bit.ly/7cl_tools_for_data_science*) To my surprise, the blog post got quite a bit of attention and I received a lot of suggestions of other command-line tools. I started wondering whether I could turn this blog post into a book. I'm pleased that, some 10 months later, with the help of many talented people (see the "Acknowledgments" on page 16 below), I was able to do just that.

I'm sharing this personal story not so much because I think you should know how this book came about, but more because I want you to know that *I* had to learn about the command line as well. Because the command line is so different from using a graphical user interface, it can be intimidating at first. But if I can learn it, then you can as well. No matter what your current operating system is and no matter how you currently do data science, by the end of this book you will be able to also leverage the power of the command line. If you're already familiar with the command line, or even if you're already dreaming in shell scripts, chances are that you'll still discover a few interesting tricks or command-line tools to use for your next data science project.

What to Expect from This Book

In this book, we're going to obtain, scrub, explore, and model data—a lot of it. This book is not so much about how to become *better* at those data science tasks. There are already great resources available that discuss, for example, when to apply which statistical test or how data can be best visualized. Instead, this practical book aims to make you more *efficient* and more *productive* by teaching you how to perform those data science tasks at the command line.

While this book discusses over 80 command-line tools, it's not the tools themselves that matter most. Some command-line tools have been around for a very long time, while others are fairly new and might eventually be replaced by better ones. There are even command-line tools that are being created as you're reading this. In the past 10 months, I have discovered many amazing command-line tools. Unfortunately, some of them were discovered too late to be included in the book. In short, command-line tools come and go, and that's OK.

What matters most are the underlying ideas of working with tools, pipes, and data. Most of the command-line tools do one thing and do it well. This is part of the Unix philosophy, which makes several appearances throughout the book. Once you become familiar with the command line, and learn how to combine command-line tools, you will have developed an invaluable skill—and if you can create new tools, you'll be a cut above.

How to Read This Book

In general, you're advised to read this book in a linear fashion. Once a concept or command-line tool has been introduced, chances are that we employ it in a later chapter. For example, in Chapter 9, we make use of `parallel`, which is discussed extensively in Chapter 8.

Data science is a broad field that intersects with many other fields, such as programming, data visualization, and machine learning. As a result, this book touches on many interesting topics that unfortunately cannot be discussed at full length. Throughout the book, there are suggestions for additional reading. It's not required to read this material in order to follow along with the book, but when you are interested, you can use turn to these suggested readings as jumping-off points.

Who This Book Is For

This book makes just one assumption about you: that you work with data. It doesn't matter which programming language or statistical computing environment you're currently using. The book explains all the necessary concepts from the beginning.

It also doesn't matter whether your operating system is Microsoft Windows, Mac OS X, or some other form of Unix. The book comes with the Data Science Toolbox, which is an easy-to-install virtual environment. It allows you to run the command-line tools and follow along with the code examples in the same environment as this book was written. You don't have to waste time figuring out how to install all the command-line tools and their dependencies.

The book contains some code in Bash, Python, and R, so it's helpful if you have some programming experience, but it's by no means required to follow along.

Conventions Used in This Book

The following typographical conventions are used in this book:

Italic
> Indicates new terms, URLs, email addresses, filenames, and file extensions.

`Constant width`
> Used for program listings, as well as within paragraphs to refer to program elements such as variable or function names, databases, data types, environment variables, statements, and keywords.

`Constant width bold`
> Shows commands or other text that should be typed literally by the user.

`Constant width italic`
> Shows text that should be replaced with user-supplied values or by values determined by context.

This element signifies a tip or suggestion.

This element signifies a general note.

This element signifies a warning or caution.

Using Code Examples

Supplemental material (virtual machine, data, scripts, and custom command-line tools, etc.) is available for download at *https://github.com/jeroenjanssens/data-science-at-the-command-line*.

This book is here to help you get your job done. In general, if example code is offered with this book, you may use it in your programs and documentation. You do not need to contact us for permission unless you're reproducing a significant portion of the code. For example, writing a program that uses several chunks of code from this book does not require permission. Selling or distributing a CD-ROM of examples from O'Reilly books does require permission. Answering a question by citing this book and quoting example code does not require permission. Incorporating a significant amount of example code from this book into your product's documentation does require permission.

We appreciate, but do not require, attribution. An attribution usually includes the title, author, publisher, and ISBN. For example: "*Data Science at the Command Line* by Jeroen H.M. Janssens (O'Reilly). Copyright 2015 Jeroen H.M. Janssens, 978-1-491-94785-2."

If you feel your use of code examples falls outside fair use or the permission given above, feel free to contact us at *permissions@oreilly.com*.

Safari® Books Online

Safari Books Online is an on-demand digital library that delivers expert content in both book and video form from the world's leading authors in technology and business.

Technology professionals, software developers, web designers, and business and creative professionals use Safari Books Online as their primary resource for research, problem solving, learning, and certification training.

Safari Books Online offers a range of plans and pricing for enterprise, government, education, and individuals.

Members have access to thousands of books, training videos, and prepublication manuscripts in one fully searchable database from publishers like O'Reilly Media, Prentice Hall Professional, Addison-Wesley Professional, Microsoft Press, Sams, Que, Peachpit Press, Focal Press, Cisco Press, John Wiley & Sons, Syngress, Morgan Kaufmann, IBM Redbooks, Packt, Adobe Press, FT Press, Apress, Manning, New Riders, McGraw-Hill, Jones & Bartlett, Course Technology, and hundreds more. For more information about Safari Books Online, please visit us online.

How to Contact Us

We have a web page for this book, where we list *non-code-related errata* and additional information. You can access this page at:

> *http://datascienceatthecommandline.com*

Any errata related to the code, command-line tools, and virtual machine should be submitted as a ticket through GitHub's issue tracker at:

> *https://github.com/jeroenjanssens/data-science-at-the-command-line/issues*

Please address comments and questions concerning this book to the publisher:

O'Reilly Media, Inc.
1005 Gravenstein Highway North
Sebastopol, CA 95472
800-998-9938 (in the United States or Canada)
707-829-0515 (international or local)
707-829-0104 (fax)

To comment or ask technical questions about this book, send email to *bookquestions@oreilly.com*.

For more information about our books, courses, conferences, and news, see our website at *http://www.oreilly.com*.

Find us on Facebook: *http://facebook.com/oreilly*

Follow us on Twitter: *http://twitter.com/oreillymedia*

Watch us on YouTube: *http://www.youtube.com/oreillymedia*

Follow Jeroen on Twitter: @jeroenhjanssens

Acknowledgments

First of all, I'd like to thank Mike Dewar and Mike Loukides for believing that my blog post, "Seven Command-Line Tools for Data Science," which I wrote in September 2013, could be expanded into a book. I thank Jared Lander for inviting me to speak at the New York Open Statistical Programming Meetup, because the preparations gave me the idea for writing the blog post in the first place.

Special thanks to my technical reviewers Mike Dewar, Brian Eoff, and Shane Reustle for reading various drafts, meticulously testing all the commands, and providing invaluable feedback. Your efforts have improved the book greatly. The remaining errors are entirely my own responsibility.

I had the privilege of working together with four amazing editors, namely: Ann Spencer, Julie Steele, Marie Beaugureau, and Matt Hacker. Thank you for your guidance and for being such great liaisons with the many talented people at O'Reilly. Those people include: Huguette Barriere, Sophia DeMartini, Dan Fauxsmith, Yasmina Greco, Rachel James, Jasmine Kwityn, Ben Lorica, Mike Loukides, Andrew Odewahn, and Christopher Pappas. There are many others whom I haven't met yet because they are operating behind the scenes. Together they ensured that working with O'Reilly has truly been a pleasure.

This book discusses over 80 command-line tools. Needless to say, without these tools, this book wouldn't have existed in the first place. I'm therefore extremely grateful to all the authors who created and contributed to these tools. The complete list of authors is unfortunately too long to include here; they are mentioned in Appendix A. Thanks especially to Aaron Crow, Jehiah Czebotar, Christopher Groskopf, Dima Kogan, Sergey Lisitsyn, Francisco J. Martin, and Ole Tange for providing help with their amazing command-line tools.

This book makes heavy use of the Data Science Toolbox, a virtual environment that contains all the command-line tools used in this book. It stands on the shoulders of many giants, and as such, I thank the people behind GNU, Linux, Ubuntu, Amazon Web Services, GitHub, Packer, Ansible, Vagrant, and VirtualBox for making the Data Science Toolbox possible. I thank Matthew Russell for the inspiration and feedback for developing the Data Science Toolbox in the first place; his book *Mining the Social Web* (O'Reilly) also offers a virtual machine.

Eric Postma and Jaap van den Herik, who supervised me during my PhD program, deserve a special thank you. Over the course of five years they have taught me many lessons. Although writing a technical book is quite different from writing a PhD thesis, many of those lessons proved to be very helpful in the past 10 months as well.

Finally, I'd like to thank my colleagues at YPlan, my friends, my family, and especially my wife, Esther, for supporting me and for disconnecting me from the command line at just the right times.

CHAPTER 1

Introduction

This book is about doing data science at the command line. Our aim is to make you a more efficient and productive data scientist by teaching you how to leverage the power of the command line.

Having both the terms "data science" and "command line" in the title requires an explanation. How can a technology that's over 40 years old[1] be of any use to a field that's only a few years young?

Today, data scientists can choose from an overwhelming collection of exciting technologies and programming languages. Python, R, Hadoop, Julia, Pig, Hive, and Spark are but a few examples. You may already have experience in one or more of these. If so, then why should you still care about the command line for doing data science? What does the command line have to offer that these other technologies and programming languages do not?

These are all valid questions. This first chapter will answer these questions as follows. First, we provide a practical definition of data science that will act as the backbone of this book. Second, we'll list five important advantages of the command line. Third, we demonstrate the power and flexibility of the command line through a real-world use case. By the end of this chapter we hope to have convinced you that the command line is indeed worth learning for doing data science.

---

1 The development of the UNIX operating system started back in 1969 (*http://www.unix.org/what_is_unix/history_timeline.html*). It featured a command line since the beginning, and the important concept of pipes was added in 1973.

Overview

In this chapter, you'll learn:

- A practical definition of data science
- What the command line is exactly and how you can use it
- Why the command line is a wonderful environment for doing data science

Data Science Is OSEMN

The field of data science is still in its infancy, and as such, there exist various definitions of what it encompasses. Throughout this book we employ a very practical definition by Mason & Wiggins (2010). They define data science according to the following five steps: (1) obtaining data, (2) scrubbing data, (3) exploring data, (4) modeling data, and (5) interpreting data. Together, these steps form the OSEMN model (which is pronounced as *awesome*). This definition serves as the backbone of this book because each step, (except step 5, interpreting data) has its own chapter. The following five subsections explain what each step entails.

 Although the five steps are discussed in a linear and incremental fashion, in practice it is very common to move back and forth between them or to perform multiple steps at the same time. Doing data science is an iterative and nonlinear process. For example, once you have modeled your data, and you look at the results, you may decide to go back to the scrubbing step to adjust the features of the data set.

Obtaining Data

Without any data, there is little data science you can do. So the first step is to obtain data. Unless you are fortunate enough to already possess data, you may need to do one or more of the following:

- Download data from another location (e.g., a web page or server)
- Query data from a database or API (e.g., MySQL or Twitter)
- Extract data from another file (e.g., an HTML file or spreadsheet)
- Generate data yourself (e.g., reading sensors or taking surveys)

In Chapter 3, we discuss several methods for obtaining data using the command line. The obtained data will most likely be in either plain text, CSV, JSON, or HTML/XML format. The next step is to scrub this data.

Scrubbing Data

It is not uncommon that the obtained data has missing values, inconsistencies, errors, weird characters, or uninteresting columns. In that case, you have to *scrub*, or clean, the data before you can do anything interesting with it. Common scrubbing operations include:

- Filtering lines
- Extracting certain columns
- Replacing values
- Extracting words
- Handling missing values
- Converting data from one format to another

While we data scientists love to create exciting data visualizations and insightful models (steps 3 and 4), usually much effort goes into obtaining and scrubbing the required data first (steps 1 and 2). In "Data Jujitsu," (*http://bit.ly/Data-Jujitsu*) DJ Patil states that "80% of the work in any data project is in cleaning the data" (2012). In Chapter 5, we demonstrate how the command line can help accomplish such data scrubbing operations.

Exploring Data

Once you have scrubbed your data, you are ready to explore it. This is where it gets interesting, because here you will get really into your data. In Chapter 7, we show you how the command line can be used to:

- Look at your data.
- Derive statistics from your data.
- Create interesting visualizations.

Command-line tools introduced in Chapter 7 include `csvstat` (Groskopf, 2014), `feedgnuplot` (Kogan, 2014), and `Rio` (Janssens, 2014).

Modeling Data

If you want to explain the data or predict what will happen, you probably want to create a statistical model of your data. Techniques to create a model include clustering, classification, regression, and dimensionality reduction. The command line is not suitable for implementing a new model from scratch. It is, however, very useful to be able to build a model from the command line. In Chapter 9, we will introduce several command-line tools that either build a model locally or employ an API to perform the computation in the cloud.

Interpreting Data

The final and perhaps most important step in the OSEMN model is interpreting data. This step involves:

- Drawing conclusions from your data
- Evaluating what your results mean
- Communicating your result

To be honest, the computer is of little use here, and the command line does not really come into play at this stage. Once you have reached this step, it is up to you. This is the only step in the OSEMN model that does not have its own chapter. Instead, we kindly refer you to *Thinking with Data (http://bit.ly/thinking-with-data)* by Max Shron (O'Reilly, 2014).

Intermezzo Chapters

In between the chapters that cover the OSEMN steps, there are three intermezzo chapters. Each intermezzo chapter discusses a more general topic concerning data science, and how the command line is employed for that. These topics are applicable to any step in the data science process.

In Chapter 4, we discuss how to create reusable tools for the command line. These personal tools can come from both long commands that you have typed on the command line, or from existing code that you have written in, say, Python or R. Being able to create your own tools allows you to become more efficient and productive.

Because the command line is an interactive environment for doing data science, it can become challenging to keep track of your workflow. In Chapter 6, we demonstrate a command-line tool called Drake (Factual, 2014), which allows you to define your data science workflow in terms of tasks and the dependencies between them. This tool increases the reproducibility of your workflow, not only for you but also for your colleagues and peers.

 In Chapter 8, we explain how your commands and tools can be sped up by running them in parallel. Using a command-line tool called GNU Parallel (Tange, 2014), we can apply command-line tools to very large data sets and run them on multiple cores and remote machines.

What Is the Command Line?

Before we discuss *why* you should use the command line for data science, let's take a peek at *what* the command line actually looks like (it may already be familiar to you). Figures 1-1 and 1-2 show a screenshot of the command line as it appears by default on Mac OS X and Ubuntu, respectively. Ubuntu is a particular distribution of GNU/Linux, which we'll be assuming throughout the book.

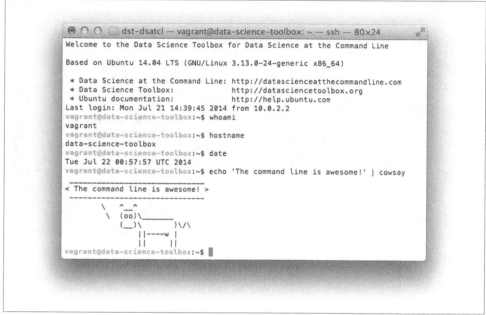

Figure 1-1. Command line on Mac OS X

The window shown in the two screenshots is called the terminal. This is the program that enables you to interact with the shell. It is the shell that executes the commands we type in. (On both Ubuntu and Mac OS X, the default shell is Bash.)

 We're not showing the Microsoft Windows command line (also known as the Command Prompt or PowerShell), because it's fundamentally different and incompatible with the commands presented in this book. The good news is that you can install the Data Science Toolbox on Microsoft Windows, so that you're still able to follow along. How to install the Data Science Toolbox is explained in Chapter 2.

Typing commands is a very different way of interacting with your computer than through a graphical user interface. If you are mostly used to processing data in, say,

Microsoft Excel, then this approach may seem intimidating at first. Don't be afraid. Trust us when we say that you'll get used to working at the command line very quickly.

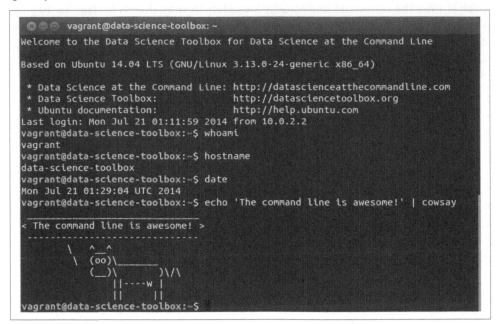

Figure 1-2. Command line on Ubuntu

In this book, the commands that we type in, and the output that they generate, is displayed as text. For example, the contents of the terminal (after the welcome message) in the two screenshots would look like this:

```
$ whoami
vagrant
$ hostname
data-science-toolbox
$ date
Tue Jul 22 02:52:09 UTC 2014
$ echo 'The command line is awesome!' | cowsay
 _____
< The command line is awesome! >
 ------------------------------
        \   ^__^
         \  (oo)_____
            (__)\       )\/\
                ||----w |
                ||     ||
```

You'll also notice that each command is preceded with a dollar sign ($). This is called the prompt. The prompt in the two screenshots showed more information, namely the username (`vagrant`), the hostname (`data-science-toolbox`), and the current working directory (`~`). It's a convention to show only a dollar sign in examples, because the prompt (1) can change during a session (when you go to a different directory), (2) can be customized by the user (e.g., it can also show the time or the current `git` (Torvalds & Hamano, 2014) branch you're working on), and (3) is irrelevant for the commands themselves.

In the next chapter we'll explain much more about essential command-line concepts. Now it's time to first explain *why* you should learn to use the command line for doing data science.

Why Data Science at the Command Line?

The command line has many great advantages that can really make you a more an efficient and productive data scientist. Roughly grouping the advantages, the command line is: agile, augmenting, scalable, extensible, and ubiquitous. We elaborate on each advantage below.

The Command Line Is Agile

The first advantage of the command line is that it allows you to be agile. Data science has a very interactive and exploratory nature, and the environment that you work in needs to allow for that. The command line achieves this by two means.

First, the command line provides a so-called read-eval-print-loop (REPL). This means that you type in a command, press **<Enter>**, and the command is evaluated immediately. A REPL is often much more convenient for doing data science than the edit-compile-run-debug cycle associated with scripts, large programs, and, say, Hadoop jobs. Your commands are executed immediately, may be stopped at will, and can be changed quickly. This short iteration cycle really allows you to play with your data.

Second, the command line is very close to the filesystem. Because data is the main ingredient for doing data science, it is important to be able to easily work with the files that contain your data set. The command line offers many convenient tools for this.

The Command Line Is Augmenting

Whatever technology your data science workflow currently includes (whether it's R, IPython, or Hadoop), you should know that we're not suggesting you abandon that workflow. Instead, the command line is presented here as an augmenting technology that amplifies the technologies you're currently employing.

The command line integrates well with other technologies. On the one hand, you can often employ the command line from your own environment. Python and R, for instance, allow you to run command-line tools and capture their output. On the other hand, you can turn your code (e.g., a Python or R function that you have already written) into a command-line tool. We will cover this extensively in Chapter 4. Moreover, the command line can easily cooperate with various databases and file types such as Microsoft Excel.

In the end, every technology has its advantages and disadvantages (including the command line), so it's good to know several and use whichever is most appropriate for the task at hand. Sometimes that means using R, sometimes the command line, and sometimes even pen and paper. By the end of this book, you'll have a solid understanding of when you could use the command line, and when you're better off continuing with your favorite programming language or statistical computing environment.

The Command Line Is Scalable

Working on the command line is very different from using a graphical user interface (GUI). On the command line you do things by typing, whereas with a GUI, you do things by pointing and clicking with a mouse.

Everything that you type manually on the command line, can also be automated through scripts and tools. This makes it very easy to re-run your commands in case you made a mistake, when the data set changed, or because your colleague wants to perform the same analysis. Moreover, your commands can be run at specific intervals, on a remote server, and in parallel on many chunks of data (more on that in Chapter 8).

Because the command line is automatable, it becomes scalable and repeatable. It is not straightforward to automate pointing and clicking, which makes a GUI a less suitable environment for doing scalable and repeatable data science.

The Command Line Is Extensible

The command line itself was invented over 40 years ago. Its core functionality has largely remained unchanged, but the *tools*, which are the workhorses of the command line, are being developed on a daily basis.

The command line itself is language agnostic. This allows the command-line tools to be written in many different programming languages. The open source community is producing many free and high-quality command-line tools that we can use for data science.

These command-line tools can work together, which makes the command line very flexible. You can also create your own tools, allowing you to extend the effective functionality of the command line.

The Command Line Is Ubiquitous

Because the command line comes with any Unix-like operating system, including Ubuntu and Mac OS X, it can be found on many computers. According to an article on Top 500 Supercomputer Sites (*http://top500.org/blog/lists/2013/11/press-release*), 95% of the top 500 supercomputers are running GNU/Linux. So, if you ever get your hands on one of those supercomputers (or if you ever find yourself in Jurassic Park with the door locks not working), you better know your way around the command line!

But GNU/Linux doesn't only run on supercomputers. It also runs on servers, laptops, and embedded systems. These days, many companies offer cloud computing, where you can easily launch new machines on the fly. If you ever log in to such a machine (or a server in general), there's a good chance that you'll arrive at the command line.

Besides mentioning that the command line is available in a lot of places, it is also important to note that the command line is not a hype. This technology has been around for more than four decades, and we're personally convinced that it's here to stay for another four. Learning how to use the command line (for data science) is therefore a worthwhile investment.

A Real-World Use Case

In the previous sections, we've given you a definition of data science and explained to you why the command line can be a great environment for doing data science. Now it's time to demonstrate the power and flexibility of the command line through a real-world use case. We'll go pretty fast, so don't worry if some things don't make sense yet.

Personally, we never seem to remember when Fashion Week is happening in New York. We know it's held twice a year, but every time it comes as a surprise! In this section we'll consult the wonderful web API of *The New York Times* to figure out when it's being held. Once you have obtained your own API keys on the developer website (*http://developer.nytimes.com*), you'll be able to, for example, search for articles, get the list of best sellers, and see a list of events.

The particular API endpoint that we're going to query is the article search one. We expect that a spike in the amount of coverage in *The New York Times* about New York Fashion Week indicates whether it's happening. The results from the API are paginated, which means that we have to execute the same query multiple times but with a different page number. (It's like clicking Next on a search engine.) This is where GNU

Parallel (Tange, 2014) comes in handy because it can act as a for loop. The entire command looks as follows (don't worry about all the command-line arguments given to parallel; we're going to discuss this in great detail in Chapter 8):

```
$ cd ~/book/ch01/data
$ parallel -j1 --progress --delay 0.1 --results results "curl -sL "\
> "'http://api.nytimes.com/svc/search/v2/articlesearch.json?q=New+York+'"\
> "'Fashion+Week&begin_date={1}0101&end_date={1}1231&page={2}&api-key='"\
> "'<your-api-key>'" ::: {2009..2013} ::: {0..99} > /dev/null

Computers / CPU cores / Max jobs to run
1:local / 4 / 1

Computer:jobs running/jobs completed/%of started jobs/Average seconds to
complete
local:1/9/100%/0.4s
```

Basically, we're performing the same query for years 2009-2014. The API only allows up to 100 pages (starting at 0) per query, so we're generating 100 numbers using brace expansion. These numbers are used by the *page* parameter in the query. We're searching for articles in 2013 that contain the search term New+York+Fashion+Week. Because the API has certain limits, we ensure that there's only one request at a time, with a one-second delay between them. Make sure that you replace <your-api-key> with your own API key for the article search endpoint.

Each request returns 10 articles, so that's 1000 articles in total. These are sorted by page views, so this should give us a good estimate of the coverage. The results are in JSON format, which we store in the *results* directory. The command-line tool tree (Baker, 2014) gives an overview of how the subdirectories are structured:

```
$ tree results | head
results
└── 1
    ├── 2009
    │   └── 2
    │       ├── 0
    │       │   ├── stderr
    │       │   └── stdout
    │       ├── 1
    │       │   ├── stderr
    │       │   └── stdout
```

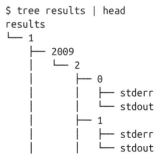

We can combine and process the results using cat (Granlund & Stallman, 2012), jq (Dolan, 2014), and json2csv (Czebotar, 2014):

```
$ cat results/1/*/2/*/stdout |                                      ❶
> jq -c '.response.docs[] | {date: .pub_date, type: .document_type, '\   ❷
> 'title: .headline.main }' | json2csv -p -k date,type,title > fashion.csv ❸
```

Let's break down this command:

❶ We combine the output of each of the 500 `parallel` jobs (or API requests).

❷ We use `jq` to extract the publication date, the document type, and the headline of each article.

❸ We convert the JSON data to CSV using `json2csv` and store it as *fashion.csv*.

With `wc -l` (Rubin & MacKenzie, 2012), we find out that this data set contains 4,855 articles (and not 5,000 because we probably retrieved everything from 2009):

```
$ wc -l fashion.csv
4856 fashion.csv
```

Let's inspect the first 10 articles to verify that we have succeeded in obtaining the data. Note that we're applying `cols` (Janssens, 2014) and `cut` (Ihnat, MacKenzie, & Meyering, 2012) to the *date* column in order to leave out the time and time zone information in the table:

```
$ < fashion.csv cols -c date cut -dT -f1 | head | csvlook
|--------------+------------+-------------------------------------------|
| date         | type       | title                                     |
|--------------+------------+-------------------------------------------|
|  2009-02-15  | multimedia | Michael Kors                              |
|  2009-02-20  | multimedia | Recap: Fall Fashion Week, New York        |
|  2009-09-17  | multimedia | UrbanEye: Backstage at Marc Jacobs        |
|  2009-02-16  | multimedia | Bill Cunningham on N.Y. Fashion Week      |
|  2009-02-12  | multimedia | Alexander Wang                            |
|  2009-09-17  | multimedia | Fashion Week Spring 2010                  |
|  2009-09-11  | multimedia | Of Color | Diversity Beyond the Runway    |
|  2009-09-14  | multimedia | A Designer Reinvents Himself              |
|  2009-09-12  | multimedia | On the Street | Catwalk                   |
|--------------+------------+-------------------------------------------|
```

That seems to have worked! In order to gain any insight, we'd better visualize the data. Figure 1-3 contains a line graph created with R (R Foundation for Statistical Computing, 2014), Rio (Janssens, 2014), and ggplot2 (Wickham, 2009).

```
$ < fashion.csv Rio -ge 'g + geom_freqpoly(aes(as.Date(date), color=type), '\
> 'binwidth=7) + scale_x_date() + labs(x="date", title="Coverage of New York'\
> ' Fashion Week in New York Times")' | display
```

By looking at the line graph, we can infer that New York Fashion Week happens two times per year. And now we know when: once in February and once in September. Let's hope that it's going to be the same this year so that we can prepare ourselves! In any case, we hope that with this example, we've shown that *The New York Times* API is an interesting source of data. More importantly, we hope that we've convinced you that the command line can be a very powerful approach for doing data science.

In this section, we've peeked at some important concepts and some exciting command-line tools. Don't worry if some things don't make sense yet. Most of the concepts will be discussed in Chapter 2, and in the subsequent chapters we'll go into more detail for all the command-line tools used in this section.

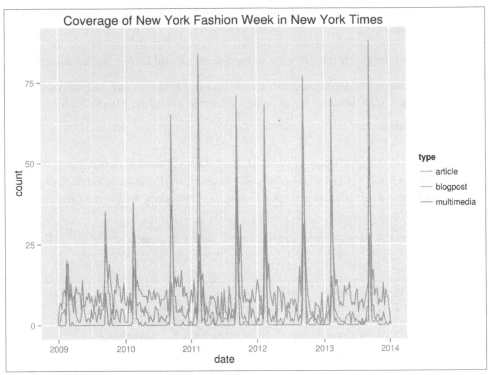

Figure 1-3. Coverage of New York Fashion Week in The New York Times

Further Reading

- Mason, H., & Wiggins, C. H. (2010). A Taxonomy of Data Science. Retrieved May 10, 2014, from *http://www.dataists.com/2010/09/a-taxonomy-of-data-science*.
- Patil, D (2012). Data Jujitsu. O'Reilly Media.
- O'Neil, C., & Schutt, R. (2013). *Doing Data Science*. O'Reilly Media.
- Shron, M. (2014). *Thinking with Data*. O'Reilly Media.

## CHAPTER 2

Getting Started

In this chapter, we are going to make sure that you have all the prerequisites for doing data science at the command line. The prerequisites fall into two parts: (1) having a proper environment with all the command-line tools that we employ in this book, and (2) understanding the essential concepts that come into play when using the command line.

First, we describe how to install the Data Science Toolbox, which is a virtual environment based on GNU/Linux that contains all the necessary command-line tools. Subsequently, we explain the essential command-line concepts through examples.

By the end of this chapter, you'll have everything you need in order to continue with the first step of doing data science, namely obtaining data.

Overview

In this chapter, you'll learn:

- How to set up the Data Science Toolbox
- Essential concepts and tools necessary to do data science at the command line

Setting Up Your Data Science Toolbox

In this book we use many different command-line tools. The distribution of GNU/Linux that we are using, Ubuntu, comes with a whole bunch of command-line tools pre-installed. Moreover, Ubuntu offers many packages that contain other, relevant command-line tools. Installing these packages yourself is not too difficult. However, we also use command-line tools that are not available as packages and require a more manual, and more involved, installation. In order to acquire the necessary command-line tools without having to go through the involved installation process of each, we encourage you to install the Data Science Toolbox.

 If you prefer to run the command-line tools natively rather than inside a virtual machine, then you can install the command-line tools individually. However, be aware that this is a very time-consuming process. Appendix A lists all the command-line tools used in the book. The installation instructions are for Ubuntu only, so check the book's website (*http://datascienceatthecommand line.com*) for up-to-date information on how to install the command-line tools natively on other operating systems. The scripts and data sets used in the book can be obtained by cloning this book's GitHub repository (*http://bit.ly/data_science_cl*).

The Data Science Toolbox is a virtual environment that allows you to get started doing data science in minutes. The default version comes with commonly used software for data science, including the Python scientific stack and R together with its most popular packages. Additional software and data bundles are easily installed. These bundles can be specific to a certain book, course, or organization. You can read more about the Data Science Toolbox at its website (*http://datasciencetoolbox.org*).

There are two ways to set up the Data Science Toolbox: (1) installing it locally using VirtualBox and Vagrant or (2) launching it in the cloud using Amazon Web Services. Both ways result in exactly the same environment. In this chapter, we explain how to set up the Data Science Toolbox for Data Science at the Command Line locally. If you wish to run the Data Science Toolbox in the cloud or if you run into problems, refer to the book's website (*http://datasciencatthecommandline.com*).

The easiest way to install the Data Science Toolbox is on your local machine. Because the local version of the Data Science Toolbox runs on top of VirtualBox and Vagrant, it can be installed on Linux, Mac OS X, and Microsoft Windows.

Step 1: Download and Install VirtualBox

Browse to the VirtualBox (Oracle, 2014) download page (*https://www.virtualbox.org/ wiki/Downloads*) and download the appropriate binary for your operating system. Open the binary and follow the installation instructions.

Step 2: Download and Install Vagrant

Similar to Step 1, browse to the Vagrant (HashiCorp, 2014) download page (*http:// www.vagrantup.com/downloads.html*) and download the appropriate binary. Open the binary and follow the installation instructions. If you already have Vagrant installed, please make sure that it's version 1.5 or higher.

Step 3: Download and Start the Data Science Toolbox

Open a terminal (known as the Command Prompt or PowerShell in Microsoft Windows). Create a directory, e.g., *MyDataScienceToolbox*, and navigate to it by typing:

```
$ mkdir MyDataScienceToolbox
$ cd MyDataScienceToolbox
```

In order to initialize the Data Science Toolbox, run the following command:

```
$ vagrant init data-science-toolbox/data-science-at-the-command-line
```

This creates a file named *Vagrantfile*. This is a configuration file that tells Vagrant how to launch the virtual machine. This file contains a lot of lines that are commented out. A minimal version is shown in Example 2-1.

Example 2-1. Minimal configuration for Vagrant

```
Vagrant.configure(2) do |config|
  config.vm.box = "data-science-toolbox/data-science-at-the-command-line"
end
```

By running the following command, the Data Science Toolbox will be downloaded and booted:

```
$ vagrant up
```

If everything went well, then you now have a Data Science Toolbox running on your local machine.

 If you ever see the message default: Warning: Connection time out. Retrying... printed repeatedly, then it may be that the virtual machine is waiting for input. This may happen when the virtual machine has not been properly shut down. In order to find out what's wrong, add the following lines to *Vagrantfile* before the last end statement (also see Example 2-2):

```
config.vm.provider "virtualbox" do |vb|
  vb.gui = true
end
```

This will cause VirtualBox to show a screen. Once the virtual machine has booted and you have identified the problem, you can remove these lines from *Vagrantfile*. The username and password to log in are both vagrant. If this doesn't help, we advise you to check the book's website (*http://datascienceatthecommandline.com*), as this website contains an up-to-date list of frequently asked questions.

Example 2-2 shows a slightly more elaborate *Vagrantfile*. You can view more configuration options at *http://docs.vagrantup.com*.

Example 2-2. Configuring Vagrant

```
Vagrant.require_version ">= 1.5.0"                                           ❶
Vagrant.configure(2) do |config|
  config.vm.box = "data-science-toolbox/data-science-at-the-command-line"
  config.vm.network "forwarded_port", guest: 8000, host: 8000               ❷
  config.vm.provider "virtualbox" do |vb|
    vb.gui = true                                                           ❸
    vb.memory = 2048                                                        ❹
    vb.cpus = 2                                                             ❺
  end
end
```

❶ Require at least version 1.5.0 of Vagrant.

❷ Forward port 8000. This is useful if you want to view a figure you created, as we do in Chapter 7.

❸ Launch a graphical user interface.

❹ Use 2 GB of memory.

❺ Use 2 CPUs.

Step 4: Log In (on Linux and Mac OS X)

If you are running Linux, Mac OS X, or some other Unix-like operating system, you can log in to the Data Science Toolbox by running the following command in a terminal:

```
$ vagrant ssh
```

After a few seconds, you will be greeted with the following message:

```
Welcome to the Data Science Toolbox for Data Science at the Command Line

Based on Ubuntu 14.04 LTS (GNU/Linux 3.13.0-24-generic x86_64)

 * Data Science at the Command Line: http://datascienceatthecommandline.com
 * Data Science Toolbox:             http://datasciencetoolbox.org
 * Ubuntu documentation:             http://help.ubuntu.com
Last login: Tue Jul 22 19:33:16 2014 from 10.0.2.2
```

Step 4: Log In (on Microsoft Windows)

If you are running Microsoft Windows, you need to either run Vagrant with a graphical user interface (refer back to Step 2 on how to set that up) or use a third-party application in order to log in to the Data Science Toolbox. For the latter, we recommend PuTTY. Browse to the PuTTY download page (*http://www.chiark.green end.org.uk/~sgtatham/putty/download.html*) and download *putty.exe*. Run PuTTY, and enter the following values:

- Host Name (or IP address): `127.0.0.1`
- Port: 2222
- Connection type: SSH

If you want, you can save these values as a session by clicking the Save button, so that you do not need to enter these values again. Click the Open button and enter `vagrant` for both the username and the password.

Step 5: Shut Down or Start Anew

The Data Science Toolbox can be shut down by running the following command from the same directory as you ran `vagrant up`:

```
$ vagrant halt
```

In case you wish to get rid of the Data Science Toolbox and start over, you can type:

```
$ vagrant destroy
```

Then, return to the instructions for Step 3 to set up the Data Science Toolbox again.

Essential Concepts and Tools

In Chapter 1, we briefly showed you what the command line is. Now that you have your own Data Science Toolbox, we can really get started. In this section, we discuss several concepts and tools that you will need to know in order to feel comfortable doing data science at the command line. If, up to now, you have been mainly working with graphical user interfaces, this might be quite a change. But don't worry, we'll start at the beginning, and very gradually go to more advanced topics.

This section is not a complete course in GNU/Linux. We will only explain the concepts and tools that are relevant for doing data science at the command line. One of the advantages of the Data Science Toolbox is that a lot is already set up. If you wish to know more about GNU/Linux, consult "Further Reading" on page 27 at the end of this chapter.

The Environment

So you've just logged into a brand new environment. Before we do anything, it's worthwhile to get a high-level understanding of this environment. The environment is roughly defined by four layers, which we briefly discuss from the top down:

Command-line tools

First and foremost, there are the command-line tools that you work with. We use them by typing their corresponding commands. There are different types of command-line tools, which we will discuss in the next section. Examples of tools are `ls` (Stallman & MacKenzie, 2012), `cat` (Granlund & Stallman, 2012), and `jq` (Dolan, 2014).

Terminal

The terminal, which is the second layer, is the application where we type our commands in. If you see the following text:

```
$ seq 3
1
2
3
```

then you would type `seq 3` into your terminal and press **<Enter>**. (The command-line tool `seq` (Drepper, 2012) generates a sequence of numbers.) You do not type the dollar sign. It's just there to serve as a prompt and let you know that you can type this command. The text below `seq 3` is the output of the command. In Chapter 1, we showed you two screenshots of how the default terminal looks in Mac OS X and Ubuntu with various commands and their output.

Shell

The third layer is the shell. Once we have typed in our command and pressed **<Enter>**, the terminal sends that command to the shell. The shell is a program that interprets the command. The Data Science Toolbox uses Bash as the shell, but there are many others available. Once you have become a bit more proficient at the command line, you may want to look into a shell called the Z shell. It offers many additional features that can increase your productivity at the command line.

Operating system

The fourth layer is the operating system, which is GNU/Linux in our case. Linux is the name of the kernel, which is the heart of the operating system. The kernel is in direct contact with the CPU, disks, and other hardware. The kernel also executes our command-line tools. GNU, which is a recursive acronym for GNU's Not Unix, refers to a set of basic tools. The Data Science Toolbox is based on a particular Linux distribution called Ubuntu.

Executing a Command-Line Tool

Now that you have an understanding of the environment, it's high time that you try out some commands. Type the following in your terminal (without the dollar sign) and press **<Enter>**:

```
$ pwd
/home/vagrant
```

This is as simple as it gets. You just executed a command that contained a single command-line tool. The command-line tool pwd (Meyering, 2012) prints the name of the directory where you currently are. By default, when you log in, this is your home directory. You can view the contents of this directory with ls (Stallman & MacKenzie, 2012):

```
$ ls
book
```

The command-line tool cd, which is a Bash builtin, allows you to navigate to a different directory:

```
$ cd book/ch02/
$ cd data
$ pwd
/home/vagrant/book/ch02/data
$ cd ..
$ pwd
/home/vagrant/book/ch02/
```

The part after cd specifies to which directory you want to navigate to. Values that come after the command are called command-line arguments or options. The two dots refer to the parent directory. Let's try a different command:

```
$ head -n 3 data/movies.txt
Matrix
Star Wars
Home Alone
```

Here we pass three command-line arguments to head (MacKenzie & Meyering, 2012). The first one is an option. The second one is a value that belongs to the option. The third one is a filename. This particular command outputs the first three lines of the file *~/book/ch02/data/movies.txt*.

Sometimes we use commands and pipelines that are too long to fit on the page. In that case, you'll see something like the following:

```
$ echo 'Hello'\
> ' world' |
> wc
```

The greater-than sign (>) is the continuation prompt, which indicates that this line is a continuation of the previous one. A long command can be broken up with either a backslash (\) or a pipe symbol (|) . Be sure to first match any quotation marks (" and '). The following command is exactly the same as the previous one:

```
$ echo 'Hello world' | wc
```

Five Types of Command-Line Tools

We employ the term "command-line tool" a lot, but we have not yet explained what we actually mean by it. We use it as an umbrella term for *anything* that can be executed from the command line. Under the hood, each command-line tool is one of the following five types:

- A binary executable
- A shell builtin
- An interpreted script
- A shell function
- An alias

It's good to know the difference between the types. The command-line tools that come pre-installed with the Data Science Toolbox mostly comprise the first two types (binary executable and shell builtin). The other three types (interpreted script, shell function, and alias) allow us to further build up our *own* data science toolbox[1] and become more efficient and more productive data scientists.

Binary executable
> Binary executables are programs in the classical sense. A binary executable is created by compiling source code to machine code. This means that when you open the file in a text editor you cannot read its source code.

Shell builtin
> Shell builtins are command-line tools provided by the shell, which is Bash in our case. Examples include cd and help. These cannot be changed. Shell builtins may differ between shells. Like binary executables, they cannot be easily inspected or changed.

Interpreted script
> An interpreted script is a text file that is executed by a binary executable. Examples include: Python, R, and Bash scripts. One great advantage of an interpreted

---

1 Here, we do not refer to the literal Data Science Toolbox we just installed, but to having your own set of tools in a figurative sense.

script is that you can read and change it. Example 2-3 shows a script named ~/book/ch02/fac.py. This script is interpreted by Python not because of the file extension .py, but because the first line of the script specifies the binary that should execute it.

Example 2-3. Python script that computes the factorial of an integer (~/book/ch02/fac.py)

```python
#!/usr/bin/env python

def factorial(x):
    result = 1
    for i in xrange(2, x + 1):
        result *= i
    return result

if __name__ == "__main__":
    import sys
    x = int(sys.argv[1])
    print factorial(x)
```

This script computes the factorial of the integer that we pass as a command-line argument. It can be invoked from the command line as follows:

```
$ book/ch02/fac.py 5
120
```

In Chapter 4, we'll discuss in great detail how to create reusable command-line tools using interpreted scripts.

Shell function

A shell function is a function that is executed by the shell itself; in our case, it is executed by Bash. They provide similar functionality to a Bash script, but they are usually (though not necessarily) smaller than scripts. They also tend to be more personal. The following command defines a function called fac, which—just like the interpreted Python script we just looked at—computes the factorial of the integer we pass as a parameter. It does this by generating a list of numbers using seq, putting those numbers on one line with * as the delimiter using paste (Ihnat & MacKenzie, 2012), and passing this equation into bc (Nelson, 2006), which evaluates it and outputs the result:

```
$ fac() { (echo 1; seq $1) | paste -s -d\* | bc; }
$ fac 5
120
```

The file ~/.bashrc, which is a configuration file for Bash, is a good place to define your shell functions so that they are always available.

Alias

Aliases are like macros. If you often find yourself executing a certain command with the same parameters (or a part of it), you can define an alias for this. Aliases are also very useful when you continue to misspell a certain command (see his GitHub profile (*http://bit.ly/mise_chrishwiggins*) for a long list of useful aliases). The following commands define two aliases:

```
$ alias l='ls -1 --group-directories-first'
$ alias moer=more
```

Now, if you type the following on the command line, the shell will replace each alias it finds with its value:

```
$ cd ~
$ l
book
```

Aliases are simpler than shell functions as they don't allow parameters. The function `fac` could not have been defined using an alias because of the parameter. Still, aliases allow you to save lots of keystrokes. Like shell functions, aliases are often defined in *.bashrc* or *.bash_aliases* configuration files, which are located in your home directory. To see all aliases currently defined, you simply run `alias` without arguments. Try it, what do you see?

In this book, when it comes to creating new command-line tools, we'll focus mostly on the last three types: interpreted scripts, shell functions, and aliases. This is because these can easily be changed. The purpose of a command-line tool is to make your life on the command line easier, and to make you a more productive and more efficient data scientist. You can find out the type of a command-line tool with `type` (which is itself a shell builtin):

```
$ type -a pwd
pwd is a shell builtin
pwd is /bin/pwd
$ type -a cd
cd is a shell builtin
$ type -a fac
fac is a function
fac ()
{
    ( echo 1;
    seq $1 ) | paste -s -d\* | bc
}
$ type -a l
l is aliased to `ls -1 --group-directories-first'
```

As you can see, `type` returns two command-line tools for `pwd`. In that case, the first reported command-line tool is used when you type `pwd`. In the next section, we'll look at how to combine command-line tools.

Combining Command-Line Tools

Because most command-line tools adhere to the Unix philosophy, they are designed to do only one thing, and do it really well. For example, the command-line tool grep (Meyering, 2012) can filter lines, wc (Rubin & MacKenzie, 2012) can count lines, and sort (Haertel & Eggert, 2012) can sort lines. The power of the command line comes from its ability to combine these small yet powerful command-line tools. The most common way of combining command-line tools is through a so-called *pipe*. The output from the first tool is passed to the second tool. There are virtually no limits to this.

Consider, for example, the command-line tool seq, which generates a sequence of numbers. Let's generate a sequence of five numbers:

```
$ seq 5
1
2
3
4
5
```

The output of a command-line tool is by default passed on to the terminal, which displays it on our screen. We can pipe the ouput of seq to a second tool, called grep, which can be used to filter lines. Imagine that we only want to see numbers that contain a "3." We can combine seq and grep as follows:

```
$ seq 30 | grep 3
3
13
23
30
```

And if we wanted to know how many numbers between 1 and 100 contain a "3", we can use wc, which is very good at counting things:

```
$ seq 100 | grep 3 | wc -l
19
```

The -l option specifies that wc should only output the number of lines. By default it also returns the number of characters and words.

You may start to see that combining command-line tools is a very powerful concept. In the rest of the book, you'll be introduced to many more tools and the functionality they offer when combining them.

Redirecting Input and Output

We mentioned that, by default, the output of the last command-line tool in the pipeline is outputted to the terminal. You can also save this output to a file. This is called output redirection, and works as follows:

```
$ cd ~/book/ch02
$ seq 10 > data/ten-numbers
```

Here, we save the output of the seq tool to a file named *ten-numbers* in the directory *~/book/ch02/data*. If this file does not exist yet, it is created. If this file already did exist, its contents would have been overwritten. You can also append the output to a file with >>, meaning the output is put after the original contents:

```
$ echo -n "Hello" > hello-world
$ echo " World" >> hello-world
```

The tool echo simply outputs the value you specify. The -n option specifies that echo should not output a trailing newline.

Saving the output to a file is useful if you need to store intermediate results (e.g., for continuing with your analysis at a later stage). To use the contents of the file *hello-world* again, we can use cat (Granlund & Stallman, 2012), which reads a file and prints it:

```
$ cat hello-world | wc -w
2
```

(Note that the -w option indicates wc to only count words.) The same result can be achieved with the following notation:

```
$ < hello-world wc -w
2
```

This way, you are directly passing the file to the standard input of wc without running an additional process. If the command-line tool also allows files to be specified as command-line arguments, which many do, you can also do the following for wc:

```
$ wc -w hello-world
2 hello-world
```

Working with Files

As data scientists, we work with a lot of data, which is often stored in files. It's important to know how to work with files (and the directories they live in) on the command line. Every action that you can do using a graphical user interface, you can do with command-line tools (and much more). In this section, we introduce the most important ones to create, move, copy, rename, and delete files and directories.

You have already seen how we can create new files by redirecting the output with either > or >>. In case you need to move a file to a different directory, you can use mv (Parker, MacKenzie, & Meyering, 2012):

```
$ mv hello-world data
```

You can also rename files with mv:

```
$ cd data
$ mv hello-world old-file
```

You can also rename or move entire directories. In case you no longer need a file, you delete (or remove) it with rm (Rubin, MacKenzie, Stallman, & Meyering, 2012):

```
$ rm old-file
```

In case you want to remove an entire directory with all its contents, specify the -r option, which stands for recursive:

```
$ rm -r ~/book/ch02/data/old
```

In case you want to copy a file, use cp (Granlund, MacKenzie, & Meyering, 2012). This is useful for creating backups:

```
$ cp server.log server.log.bak
```

You can create directories using mkdir (MacKenzie, 2012):

```
$ cd data
$ mkdir logs
```

All of these command-line tools accept the -v option, which stands for *verbose*, so that they output what's going on. All but mkdir accept the -i option, which stands for *interactive*, and causes the tools to ask you for confirmation.

Using the command-line tools to manage your files can be scary at first, because you have no graphical overview of the filesystem to provide immediate feedback.

Help!

As you are finding your way around the command line, it may happen that you need help. Even the most-seasoned Linux users need help at some point. It's impossible to remember all the different command-line tools and their options. Fortunately, the command line offers severals ways to get help.

Perhaps the most important command to get help is perhaps man (Eaton & Watson, 2014), which is short for *manual*. It contains information for most command-line tools. Imagine that we forgot the different options to the tool cat. You can access its man page using:

```
$ man cat | head -n 20
CAT(1)                          User Commands                          CAT(1)
```

```
NAME
       cat - concatenate files and print on the standard output

SYNOPSIS
       cat [OPTION]... [FILE]...

DESCRIPTION
       Concatenate FILE(s), or standard input, to standard output.

       -A, --show-all
              equivalent to -vET

       -b, --number-nonblank
              number nonempty output lines, overrides -n

       -e     equivalent to -vE
```

 Sometimes you'll see us use head, fold, or cut at the end of a command. This is only to ensure that the output of the command fits on the page; you don't have to type these. For example, head -n 5 only prints the first five lines, fold wraps long lines to 80 characters, and cut -c1-80 trims lines that are longer than 80 characters.

Not every command-line tool has a man page. For shell builtins, such as cd, you need to use the help command-line tool:

```
$ help cd | head -n 20
cd: cd [-L|[-P [-e]] [-@]] [dir]
    Change the shell working directory.

    Change the current directory to DIR.  The default DIR is the value of the
    HOME shell variable.

    The variable CDPATH defines the search path for the directory containing
    DIR.  Alternative directory names in CDPATH are separated by a colon (:).
    A null directory name is the same as the current directory.  If DIR begins
    with a slash (/), then CDPATH is not used.

    If the directory is not found, and the shell option 'cdable_vars' is set,
    the word is assumed to be  a variable name.  If that variable has a value,
    its value is used for DIR.

    Options:
        -L      force symbolic links to be followed: resolve symbolic links in
        DIR after processing instances of '..'
        -P      use the physical directory structure without following symbolic
        links: resolve symbolic links in DIR before processing instances
```

`help` also covers other topics of Bash, in case you are interested (try `help` without command-line arguments for a list of topics).

Newer tools that can be used from the command line often lack a man page as well. In that case, your best bet is to invoke the tool with the `-h` or `--help` option. For example:

```
jq --help

jq - commandline JSON processor [version 1.4]
Usage: jq [options] <jq filter> [file...]

For a description of the command line options and
how to write jq filters (and why you might want to)
see the jq manpage, or the online documentation at
http://stedolan.github.com/jq
```

Specifying the `--help` option also works for GNU command-line tools, such as `cat`. However, the corresponding man page often provides more information. If after trying these three approaches, you're still stuck, then it's perfectly acceptable to consult the Internet. In Appendix A, there's a list of all command-line tools used in this book. Besides how each command-line tool can be installed, it also shows how you can get help.

Further Reading

- Janssens, J. H. M. (2014). Data Science Toolbox. Retrieved May 10, 2014, from *http://datasciencetoolbox.org*.
- Oracle. (2014). VirtualBox. Retrieved May 10, 2014, from *http://virtualbox.org*.
- HashiCorp. (2014). Vagrant. Retrieved May 10, 2014, from *http://vagrantup.com*.
- Heddings, L. (2006). Keyboard Shortcuts for Bash. Retrieved May 10, 2014, from *http://www.howtogeek.com/howto/ubuntu/keyboard-shortcuts-for-bash-command-shell-for-ubuntu-debian-suse-redhat-linux-etc*.
- Peek, J., Powers, S., O'Reilly, T., & Loukides, M. (2002). *Unix Power Tools* (3rd Ed.). O'Reilly Media.

## CHAPTER 3

Obtaining Data

This chapter deals with the first step of the OSEMN model: obtaining data. After all, without any data, there is not much data science that we can do. We assume that the data that is needed to solve the data science problem at hand already exists at some location in some form. Our goal is to get this data onto your computer (or into your Data Science Toolbox) in a form that we can work with.

According to the Unix philosophy, text is a universal interface. Almost every command-line tool takes text as input, produces text as output, or both. This is the main reason why command-line tools can work so well together. However, as we'll see, even just text can come in multiple forms.

Data can be obtained in several ways—for example by downloading it from a server, by querying a database, or by connecting to a web API. Sometimes, the data comes in a compressed form or in a binary format such as Microsoft Excel. In this chapter, we discuss several tools that help tackle this from the command line, including: `curl` (Stenberg, 2012), `in2csv` (Groskopf, 2014), `sql2csv` (Groskopf, 2014), and `tar` (Bailey, Eggert, & Poznyakoff, 2014).

Overview

In this chapter, you'll learn how to:

- Download data from the Internet
- Query databases
- Connect to web APIs

- Decompress files
- Convert Microsoft Excel spreadsheets into usable data

Copying Local Files to the Data Science Toolbox

A common situation is that you already have the necessary files on your own computer. This section explains how you can get those files onto the local or remote version of the Data Science Toolbox.

Local Version of Data Science Toolbox

We mentioned in Chapter 2 that the local version of the Data Science Toolbox is an isolated virtual environment. Luckily, there is one exception to that: files can be transfered in and out the Data Science Toolbox. The local directory from which you ran vagrant up (which is the one that contains the file *Vagrantfile*) is mapped to a directory in the Data Science Toolbox. This directory is called */vagrant* (note that this is not your home directory). Let's check the contents of this directory:

```
$ ls -1 /vagrant
Vagrantfile
```

If you have a file on your local computer, and you want to apply some command-line tools to it, all you have to do is copy or move the file to that directory. Let's assume that you have a file called *logs.csv* on your Desktop. If you are running GNU/Linux or Mac OS X, execute the following command on your operating system (and not inside the Data Science Toolbox) from the directory that contains *Vagrantfile*:

```
$ cp ~/Desktop/logs.csv .
```

And if you're running Windows, you can run the following on the Command Prompt or PowerShell:

```
> cd %UserProfile%\Desktop
> copy logs.csv MyDataScienceToolbox\
```

You may also drag and drop the file into the directory using Windows Explorer.

The file is now located in the directory */vagrant*. It's a good idea to keep your data in a separate directory (here we're using *~/book/ch03/data*, for example). So, after you have copied the file, you can move it by running:

```
$ mv /vagrant/logs.csv ~/book/ch03/data
```

Remote Version of Data Science Toolbox

If you are running Linux or Mac OS X, you can use scp (Rinne & Ylonen, 2014), which stands for *secure copy*, to copy files onto the EC2 instance. You will need the same key pair file that you used to log in to the EC2 instance running the Data Science Toolbox:

```
$ scp -i  mykey.pem ~/Desktop/logs.csv \
> ubuntu@ec2-184-73-72-150.compute-1.amazonaws.com:data
```

Replace the hostname in the example (the part between @ and :) with the value you see on the EC2 overview page in the AWS console.

Decompressing Files

If the original data set is very large or it's a collection of many files, the file may be a (compressed) archive. Data sets which contain many repeated values (such as the words in a text file or the keys in a JSON file) are especially well suited for compression.

Common file extensions of compressed archives are: *.tar.gz*, *.zip*, and *.rar*. To decompress these, you would use the command-line tools tar (Bailey, Eggert, & Poznyakoff, 2014), unzip (Smith, 2009), and unrar (Asselstine, Scheurer, & Winkelmann, 2014), respectively. There are a few more, though less common, file extensions for which you would need yet other tools. For example, in order to extract a file named *logs.tar.gz*, you would use:

```
$ cd ~/book/ch03
$ tar -xzvf data/logs.tar.gz
```

Indeed, tar is notorious for its many options. In this case, the four options x, z, v, and f specify that tar should *extract* files from an archive, use *gzip* as the decompression algorithm, be *verbose*, and use the file *logs.tar.gz*. In time you'll get used to typing these four characters, but there's a more convenient way.

Rather than remembering the different command-line tools and their options, there's a handy script called unpack (Brisbin, 2013), which will decompress many different formats. unpack looks at the extension of the file that you want to decompress, and calls the appropriate command-line tool.

The unpack tool is part of the Data Science Toolbox. Remember that you can look up how it can be installed in Appendix A. Example 3-1 shows the source of unpack. Although Bash scripting is not the focus of this book, it's still useful to take a moment to figure out how it works.

Example 3-1. Decompress various file formats (unpack)

```
#!/usr/bin/env bash
# unpack: Extract common file formats

# Display usage if no parameters given
```

```
  if [[ -z "$@" ]]; then
    echo " ${0##*/} <archive> - extract common file formats)"
    exit
  fi

# Required program(s)
  req_progs=(7z unrar unzip)
  for p in ${req_progs[@]}; do
    hash "$p" 2>&- || \
    { echo >&2 " Required program \"$p\" not installed."; exit 1; }
  done

# Test if file exists
  if [ ! -f "$@" ]; then
    echo "File "$@" doesn't exist"
    exit.
  fi

# Extract file by using extension as reference
  case "$@" in
    *.7z ) 7z x "$@" ;;
    *.tar.bz2 ) tar xvjf "$@" ;;
    *.bz2 ) bunzip2 "$@" ;;
    *.deb ) ar vx "$@" ;;
    *.tar.gz ) tar xvf "$@" ;;
    *.gz ) gunzip "$@" ;;
    *.tar ) tar xvf "$@" ;;
    *.tbz2 ) tar xvjf "$@" ;;
    *.tar.xz ) tar xvf "$@" ;;
    *.tgz ) tar xvzf "$@" ;;
    *.rar ) unrar x "$@" ;;
    *.zip ) unzip "$@" ;;
    *.Z ) uncompress "$@" ;;
    * ) echo " Unsupported file format" ;;
  esac
```

Now, in order to decompress this same file, you would simply use:

```
$ unpack logs.tar.gz
```

Converting Microsoft Excel Spreadsheets

For many people, Microsoft Excel offers an intuitive way to work with small data sets and perform calculations on them. As a result, a lot of data is embedded into Microsoft Excel spreadsheets. These spreadsheets are, depending on the extension of the filename, stored in either a proprietary binary format (*.xls*) or as a collection of compressed XML files (*.xlsx*). In both cases, the data is not readily usable by most command-line tools. It would be a shame if we could not use those valuable data sets just because they are stored this way.

Luckily, there is a command-line tool called in2csv (Groskopf, 2014), which is able to convert Microsoft Excel spreadsheets to CSV files. CSV stands for comma-separated values or character-separated values. Working with CSV can be tricky because it lacks a formal specification. RFC 4180 (*http://www.ietf.org/rfc/rfc4180.txt*) defines the CSV format according to the following three points:

1. Each record is located on a separate line, delimited by a line break (CRLF). For example:

   ```
   aaa,bbb,ccc CRLF
   zzz,yyy,xxx CRLF
   ```

2. The last record in the file may or may not have an ending line break. For example:

   ```
   aaa,bbb,ccc CRLF
   zzz,yyy,xxx
   ```

3. There may be an optional header line appearing as the first line of the file with the same format as normal record lines. This header will contain names corresponding to the fields in the file and should contain the same number of fields as the records in the rest of the file (the presence or absence of the header line should be indicated via the optional header parameter of this MIME type). For example:

   ```
   field_name,field_name,field_name CRLF
   aaa,bbb,ccc CRLF
   zzz,yyy,xxx CRLF
   ```

Let's demonstrate in2csv using a spreadsheet that contains the top 250 movies from the Internet Movie Database (IMDb). The file is named *imdb-250.xlsx* and can be obtained from *http://bit.ly/analyzing_top250_movies_list*. To extract its data, we invoke in2csv as follows:

```
$ cd ~/book/ch03
$ in2csv data/imdb-250.xlsx > data/imdb-250.csv
```

The format of the file is automatically determined by the extension, *.xlsx* in this case. If we were to pipe the data into in2csv, we would have to specify the format explicitly. Let's look at the data:

```
$ in2csv data/imdb-250.xlsx | head | cut -c1-80
Title,title trim,Year,Rank,Rank (desc),Rating,New in 2011 from 2010?,2010 rank,R
Sherlock Jr. (1924),SherlockJr.(1924),1924,221,30,8,y,n/a,n/a,
The Passion of Joan of Arc (1928),ThePassionofJoanofArc(1928),1928,212,39,8,y,n/
His Girl Friday (1940),HisGirlFriday(1940),1940,250,1,8,y,n/a,n/a,
Tokyo Story (1953),TokyoStory(1953),1953,248,3,8,y,n/a,n/a,
The Man Who Shot Liberty Valance (1962),TheManWhoShotLibertyValance(1962),1962,2
Persona (1966),Persona(1966),1966,200,51,8,y,n/a,n/a,
Stalker (1979),Stalker(1979),1979,243,8,8,y,n/a,n/a,
```

```
Fanny and Alexander (1982),FannyandAlexander(1982),1982,210,41,8,y,n/a,n/a,
Beauty and the Beast (1991),BeautyandtheBeast(1991),1991,249,2,8,y,n/a,n/a,
```

As you can see, CSV by default is not too readable. You can pipe the data to a tool called csvlook (Groskopf, 2014), which will nicely format the data into a table. Here, we'll display a subset of the columns using csvcut such that the table fits on the page:

```
$ in2csv data/imdb-250.xlsx | head | csvcut -c Title,Year,Rating | csvlook
|-----------------------------------------------+------+--------|
| Title                                         | Year | Rating |
|-----------------------------------------------+------+--------|
| Sherlock Jr. (1924)                           | 1924 | 8      |
| The Passion of Joan of Arc (1928)             | 1928 | 8      |
| His Girl Friday (1940)                         | 1940 | 8      |
| Tokyo Story (1953)                            | 1953 | 8      |
| The Man Who Shot Liberty Valance (1962)       | 1962 | 8      |
| Persona (1966)                                | 1966 | 8      |
| Stalker (1979)                                | 1979 | 8      |
| Fanny and Alexander (1982)                    | 1982 | 8      |
| Beauty and the Beast (1991)                   | 1991 | 8      |
|-----------------------------------------------+------+--------|
```

A spreadsheet can contain multiple worksheets. By default, in2csv extracts the first worksheet. To extract a different worksheet, you need to pass the name of worksheet to the --sheet option.

The tools in2csv, csvcut, and csvlook are actually part of Csvkit, which is a collection of command-line tools to work with CSV data. Csvkit will be used quite often in this book because it has so many valuable tools. If you're running the Data Science Toolbox, you already have Csvkit installed. Otherwise, see Appendix A for instructions on how to install it.

 An alternative approach to in2csv is to open the spreadsheet in Microsoft Excel or an open source variant such as LibreOffice Calc, and manually export it to CSV. While this works as a one-off solution, the disadvantage is that it does not scale well to multiple files and is not automatable. Furthermore, when you are working on the command line of a remote server, chances are that you don't have such an application available.

Querying Relational Databases

Most companies store their data in a relational database. Examples of relational databases are MySQL, PostgreSQL, and SQLite. These databases all have a slightly different way of interfacing with them. Some provide a command-line tool or a command-line interface, while others do not. Moreover, they are not very consistent when it comes to their usage and output.

Fortunately, there is a command-line tool called `sql2csv`, which is part of the Csvkit suite. Because it leverages the Python SQLAlchemy package, we only have to use one tool to execute queries on many different databases, including MySQL, Oracle, PostgreSQL, SQLite, Microsoft SQL Server, and Sybase. The output of `sql2csv` is, as its name suggests, in CSV format.

We can obtain data from relational databases by executing a `SELECT` query on them. (`sql2csv` also support `INSERT`, `UPDATE`, and `DELETE` queries, but that's not the purpose of this chapter.) To select a specific set of data from an SQLite database named *iris.db*, `sql2csv` can be invoked as follows:

```
$ sql2csv --db 'sqlite:///data/iris.db' --query 'SELECT * FROM iris '\
> 'WHERE sepal_length > 7.5'
sepal_length,sepal_width,petal_length,petal_width,species
7.6,3.0,6.6,2.1,Iris-virginica
7.7,3.8,6.7,2.2,Iris-virginica
7.7,2.6,6.9,2.3,Iris-virginica
7.7,2.8,6.7,2.0,Iris-virginica
7.9,3.8,6.4,2.0,Iris-virginica
7.7,3.0,6.1,2.3,Iris-virginica
```

Here, we're selecting all rows where `sepal_length` is larger than 7.5. The `--db` option specifies the database URL, of which the typical form is: `dialect+driver://user name:password@host:port/database`.

Downloading from the Internet

The Internet provides without a doubt the largest resource for data. This data is available in various forms, using various protocols. The command-line tool cURL (Stenberg, 2012) can be considered the command line's Swiss Army knife when it comes to downloading data from the Internet.

When you access a URL, which stands for *uniform resource locator*, through your browser, the data that is downloaded can be interpreted. For example, an HTML file is rendered as a website, an MP3 file may be automatically played, and a PDF file may be automatically opened by a viewer. However, when cURL is used to access a URL, the data is downloaded as is, and is printed to standard output. Other command-line tools may then be used to process this data further.

The easiest invocation of `curl` is to simply specify a URL as a command-line argument. For example, to download Mark Twain's *Adventures of Huckleberry Finn* from Project Gutenberg, we can run the following command:

```
$ curl -s http://www.gutenberg.org/cache/epub/76/pg76.txt | head -n 10

The Project Gutenberg EBook of Adventures of Huckleberry Finn, Complete
by Mark Twain (Samuel Clemens)
```

```
This eBook is for the use of anyone anywhere at no cost and with almost
no restrictions whatsoever. You may copy it, give it away or re-use
it under the terms of the Project Gutenberg License included with this
eBook or online at www.gutenberg.net
```

By default, `curl` outputs a progress meter that shows the download rate and the
expected time of completion. If you are piping the output directly to another
command-line tool, such as `head`, be sure to specify the `-s` option, which stands for
silent, so that the progress meter is disabled. Compare, for example, the output with
the following command:

```
$ curl http://www.gutenberg.org/cache/epub/76/pg76.txt | head -n 10
  % Total    % Received % Xferd  Average Speed   Time    Time     Time  Current
                                 Dload  Upload   Total   Spent    Left  Speed

  0     0    0     0    0     0      0      0 --:--:-- --:--:-- --:--:--

The Project Gutenberg EBook of Adventures of Huckleberry Finn, Complete
by Mark Twain (Samuel Clemens)

This eBook is for the use of anyone anywhere at no cost and with almost
no restrictions whatsoever. You may copy it, give it away or re-use
it under the terms of the Project Gutenberg License included with this
eBook or online at www.gutenberg.net
```

Note that the output of the second command, where we do not disable the progress
meter, contains the unwanted text and even an error message. If you save the data to a
file, then you do not need to necessarily specify the `-s` option:

```
$ curl http://www.gutenberg.org/cache/epub/76/pg76.txt > data/finn.txt
```

You can also save the data by explicitly specifying the output file with the `-o` option:

```
$ curl -s http://www.gutenberg.org/cache/epub/76/pg76.txt -o data/finn.txt
```

When downloading data from the Internet, the URL will most likely use the protocols
HTTP or HTTPS. To download from an FTP server, which stands for *File Transfer
Protocol*, you use `curl` in exactly the same way. When the URL is password protected,
you can specify a username and a password as follows:

```
$ curl -u username:password ftp://host/file
```

If the specified URL is a directory, `curl` will list the contents of that directory.

When you access a shortened URL, such as the ones that start with *http://bit.ly/* or
http://t.co/, your browser automatically redirects you to the correct location. With
`curl`, however, you need to specify the `-L` or `--location` option in order to be redi-
rected:

```
$ curl -L j.mp/locatbbar
```

If you do not specify the `-L` or `--location` option, you may get something like:

```
$ curl j.mp/locatbbar
<html>
<head>
<title>bit.ly</title>
</head>
<body>
<a href="http://en.wikipedia.org/wiki/List_of_countries_and_territories_by_bo
rder/area_ratio">moved here</a>
</body>
```

By specifying the -I or --head option, curl fetches only the HTTP header of the response:

```
$ curl -I j.mp/locatbbar
HTTP/1.1 301 Moved Permanently
Server: nginx
Date: Wed, 21 May 2014 18:50:28 GMT
Content-Type: text/html; charset=utf-8
Connection: keep-alive
Cache-Control: private; max-age=90
Content-Length: 175
Location: http://en.wikipedia.org/wiki/List_of_countries_and_territories_by_bo
Mime-Version: 1.0
Set-Cookie: _bit=537cf574-002ba-07d79-2e1cf10a;domain=.j.mp;expires=Mon Nov 17
```

The first line indicates the HTTP status code, which is 301 (moved permanently) in this case. You can also see the location this URL redirects to: *http://en.wikipedia.org/wiki/List_of_countries_and_territories_by_border/area_ratio*. Inspecting the header and getting the status code is a useful debugging tool in case curl does not give you the expected result. Other common HTTP status codes include 404 (not found) and 403 (forbidden). (See Wikipedia (*http://bit.ly/status_codes*) for a list of all HTTP status codes.)

To conclude this section, cURL is a straightforward command-line tool for downloading data from the Internet. Its three most common options are -s to suppress the progress meter, -u to specify a username and password, and -L to automatically follow redirects. See its man page for more information.

Calling Web APIs

In the previous section we explained how to download individual files from the Internet. Another way data can come from the Internet is through a web API, which stands for *application programming interface*. The number of APIs that are being offered by organizations is growing at an ever increasing rate, which means a lot of interesting data is available for us data scientists!

Web APIs are not meant to be presented in a nice layout, such as websites. Instead, most web APIs return data in a structured format, such as JSON or XML. Having data in a structured form has the advantage that the data can be easily processed by other tools, such as `jq`. For example, the API from *http://randomuser.me* returns data in the following JSON structure:

```
$ curl -s http://api.randomuser.me | jq '.'
{
  "results": [
    {
      "version": "0.3.2",
      "seed": "1c5b868416387bf",
      "user": {
        "picture": "http://api.randomuser.me/0.3.2/portraits/women/2.jpg",
        "SSN": "972-79-4140",
        "cell": "(519)-135-8132",
        "phone": "(842)-322-2703",
        "dob": "64945368",
        "registered": "1136430654",
        "sha1": "a3fed7d4f481fbd6845c0c5a19e4f1113cc977ed",
        "gender": "female",
        "name": {
          "last": "green",
          "first": "scarlett",
          "title": "miss"
        },
        "location": {
          "zip": "43413",
          "state": "nevada",
          "city": "redding",
          "street": "8608 crescent canyon st"
        },
        "email": "scarlett.green32@example.com",
        "username": "reddog82",
        "password": "ddddd",
        "salt": "AEKvMi$+",
        "md5": "f898fc73430cff8327b91ef6d538be5b"
      }
    }
  ]
}
```

The data is piped to the `jq` command-line tool in order to display it in a nice way. `jq` has many more possibilities that we will explore in Chapter 5.

Some web APIs return data in a streaming manner. This means that once you connect to it, the data will continue to pour in forever. A well-known example is the Twitter firehose, which constantly streams all the tweets sent around the world. Luckily, most command-line tools that we use also operate in a streaming manner, so that we may also use this kind of data.

Some APIs require you to log in using the OAuth protocol. There's a convenient command-line tool called `curlicue` (Foster, 2014) that assists in performing the so-called *OAuth dance*. Once this has been set up, `curlicue` will call `curl` with the correct headers. First, you set everything up for a particular API with curlicue-setup, and then you can call that API using curlicue. For example, to use curlicue with the Twitter API, you would run:

```
$ curlicue-setup \
> 'https://api.twitter.com/oauth/request_token' \
> 'https://api.twitter.com/oauth/authorize?oauth_token=$oauth_token' \
> 'https://api.twitter.com/oauth/access_token' \
> credentials
$ curlicue -f credentials \
> 'https://api.twitter.com/1/statuses/home_timeline.xml'
```

For more popular APIs, there are specialized command-line tools available. These are wrappers that provide a convenient way to connect to the API. In Chapter 9, for example, we'll be using the command-line tool bigmler that connects to BigML's prediction API.

Further Reading

- Molinaro, A. (2005). *SQL Cookbook*. O'Reilly Media.
- Wikipedia. (2014). List of HTTP status codes. Retrieved May 10, 2014, from *http://en.wikipedia.org/wiki/List_of_HTTP_status_codes*.

## CHAPTER 4

Creating Reusable Command-Line Tools

Throughout the book, we use a lot of commands and pipelines that basically fit on one line (let's call those *one-liners*). Being able to perform complex tasks with just a one-liner is what makes the command line powerful. It's a very different experience from writing traditional programs.

Some tasks you perform only once, and some you perform more often. Some tasks are very specific and others can be generalized. If you foresee or notice that you need to repeat a certain one-liner on a regular basis, it's worthwhile to turn this into a command-line tool of its own. Both one-liners and command-line tools have their uses. Recognizing the opportunity requires practice and skill. The advantage of a command-line tool is that you don't have to remember the entire one-liner and that it improves readability if you include it into some other pipeline.

The benefit of working with a programming language is that you have the code in a file. This means that you can easily reuse that code. If the code has parameters it can even be applied to problems that follow a similar pattern.

Command-line tools have the best of both worlds: they can be used from the command line, accept parameters, and only have to be created only once. In this chapter, we're going to get familiar with creating reusable command-line tools in two ways. First, we explain how to turn one-liners into reusable command-line tools. By adding parameters to our commands, we can add the same flexibility that a programming language offers. Subsequently, we demonstrate how to create reusable command-line tools from code you've written in a programming language. By following the Unix philosophy, your code can be combined with other command-line tools, which may be written in an entirely different language. We'll focus on two programming languages: Python and R.

We believe that creating reusable command-line tools makes you a more efficient and productive data scientist in the long run. You gradually build up your own data science toolbox from which you can draw existing tools and apply it to new problems you have previously encountered in a similar form. It requires practice in order to be able to recognize the opportunity to turn a one-liner or existing code into a command-line tool.

To turn a one-liner into a shell script, we need to use some shell scripting. We'll only demonstrate the usefulness of a small subset of concepts from shell scripting. A complete course in shell scripting deserves a book of its own, and is therefore beyond the scope of this one. If you want to dive deeper into shell scripting, we recommend *Classic Shell Scripting* (*http://bit.ly/Classic_Shell_Scripting*) by Robbins & Beebe (2005).

Overview

In this chapter, you'll learn how to:

- Convert one-liners into shell scripts
- Make existing Python and R code part of the command line

Converting One-Liners into Shell Scripts

In this section, we're going to explain how to turn a one-liner into a reusable command-line tool. Imagine that we have the following one-liner:

```
$ curl -s http://www.gutenberg.org/cache/epub/76/pg76.txt |   ❶
> tr '[:upper:]' '[:lower:]' |     ❷
> grep -oE '\w+' |                 ❸
> sort |                          ❹
> uniq -c |                       ❺
> sort -nr |                      ❻
> head -n 10                      ❼
   6441 and
   5082 the
   3666 i
   3258 a
   3022 to
   2567 it
   2086 t
   2044 was
   1847 he
   1778 of
```

In short, as you may have guessed from the output, this one-liner returns the top ten words of the ebook version of *Adventures of Huckleberry Finn*. It accomplishes this by:

❶ Downloading the ebook using `curl`.

❷ Converting the entire text to lowercase using `tr` (Meyering, 2012).

❸ Extracting all the words using `grep` (Meyering, 2012) and putting each word on a separate line.

❹ Sorting these words in alphabetical order using `sort` (Haertel & Eggert, 2012).

❺ Removing all the duplicates and counting how often each word appears in the list using `uniq` (Stallman & MacKenzie, 2012).

❻ Sorting this list of unique words by their count in descending order using `sort`.

❼ Keeping only the top 10 lines (i.e., words) using `head`.

 Each command-line tool used in this one-liner offers a man page. So, in case you would like to know more about, say, `grep`, you can run `man grep` from the command line. The command-line tools `tr`, `grep`, `uniq`, and `sort` will be discussed in more detail in the next chapter.

There is nothing wrong with running this one-liner just once. However, imagine if we wanted to find the top 10 words of every ebook on Project Gutenberg. Or imagine that we wanted the top 10 words of a news website on an hourly basis. In those cases, it would be best to have this one-liner as a separate building block that can be part of something bigger. We want to add some flexibility to this one-liner in terms of parameters, so we'll turn it into a shell script.

Since we use Bash as our shell, the script will be written in the programming language Bash. This allows us to take the one-liner as the starting point, and gradually improve on it. To turn this one-liner into a reusable command-line tool, we'll walk you through the following six steps:

1. Copy and paste the one-liner into a file.
2. Add execute permissions.
3. Define a so-called shebang.
4. Remove the fixed input part.
5. Add a parameter.
6. Optionally extend your PATH.

Step 1: Copy and Paste

The first step is to create a new file. Open your favorite text editor and copy and paste our one-liner. We name the file *top-words-1.sh* (the *1* stands for the first step towards our new command-line tool) and put it in the *~/book/ch04* directory, but you may choose a different name and location. The contents of the file should look something like Example 4-1.

Example 4-1. ~/book/ch04/top-words-1.sh

```
curl -s http://www.gutenberg.org/cache/epub/76/pg76.txt |
tr '[:upper:]' '[:lower:]' | grep -oE '\w+' | sort |
uniq -c | sort -nr | head -n 10
```

We're using the file extension *.sh* to make clear that we're creating a shell script. However, command-line tools do not need to have an extension. In fact, command-line tools rarely have extensions.

> Here is a nice little command-line trick. On the command-line, !!
> will be substituted with the command you just ran. So, if you realize you needed superuser privileges for the previous command, you can run sudo !! (Miller, 2013). Moreover, if you want to save the previous command to a file without having to copy and paste it, you can run echo "!!" > scriptname. Be sure to check the contents of the file *scriptname* for correctness before executing it because it may not always work when your command has quotes.

We can now use the command-line tool bash (Fox & Ramey, 2010) to interpret and execute the commands in the file:

```
$ bash ~/book/ch04/top-words-1.sh
   6441 and
   5082 the
   3666 i
   3258 a
   3022 to
   2567 it
   2086 t
   2044 was
   1847 he
   1778 of
```

This first step already saves us from typing the one-liner the next time we want to use it. Because the file cannot be executed on its own, we cannot really speak of a true command-line tool yet. Let's change that in the next step.

Step 2: Add Permission to Execute

The reason we cannot execute our file directly is that we do not have the correct access permissions. In particular, you, as a user, need to have the permission to execute the file. In this section, we'll change the access permissions of our file.

 In order to show the differences between steps, we copy the file to *top-words-2.sh* using `cp top-words-{1,2}.sh`. You can keep working with the same file if you want to.

To change the access permissions of a file, we use a command-line tool called `chmod` (MacKenzie & Meyering, 2012), which stands for *change mode*. It changes the file mode bits of a specific file. The following command gives the user, you, the permission to execute *top-words-2.sh*:

```
$ cd ~/book/ch04/
$ chmod u+x top-words-2.sh
```

The `u+x` option consists of three characters: (1) `u` indicates that we want to change the permissions for the user who owns the file, which is you, because you created the file; (2) `+` indicates that we want to add a permission; and (3) `x`, which indicates the permissions to execute. Now let's have a look at the access permissions of both files:

```
$ ls -l top-words-{1,2}.sh
-rw-rw-r-- 1 vagrant vagrant 145 Jul 20 23:33 top-words-1.sh
-rwxrw-r-- 1 vagrant vagrant 143 Jul 20 23:34 top-words-2.sh
```

The first column shows the access permissions for each file. For *top-words-2.sh*, this is `-rwxrw-r--`. The first character, `-`, indicates the file type. A `-` means regular file and a `d` (not present here) means directory. The next three characters, `rwx`, indicate the access permissions for the user who owns the file. The `r` and `w` mean read and write, respectively. (As you can see, *top-words-1.sh* has a `-` instead of an `x`, which means that we cannot execute that file.) The next three characters, `rw-`, indicate the access permissions for all members of the group that owns the file. Finally, the last three characters in the column, `r--`, indicate access permissions for all other users.

Now you can execute the file as follows:

```
$ ~/book/ch04/top-words-2.sh
   6441 and
   5082 the
   3666 i
   3258 a
   3022 to
   2567 it
   2086 t
   2044 was
```

```
1847 he
1778 of
```

Note that if you're in the same directory as the executable, you need to execute it as follows (note the `./`):

```
$ cd ~/book/ch04
$ ./top-words-2.sh
```

If you try to execute a file for which you do not have the correct access permissions, as with *top-words-1.sh*, you'll see the following error message:

```
$ ./top-words-1.sh
bash: ./top-words-1.sh: Permission denied
```

Step 3: Define Shebang

Although we can already execute the file on its own, we should add a so-called *shebang* to the file. The shebang is a special line in the script that instructs the system which executable should be used to interpret the commands. In our case, we want to use `bash` to interpret our commands. Example 4-2 shows what the file *top-words-3.sh* looks like with a shebang.

Example 4-2. ~/book/ch04/top-words-3.sh

```
#!/usr/bin/env bash
curl -s http://www.gutenberg.org/cache/epub/76/pg76.txt |
tr '[:upper:]' '[:lower:]' | grep -oE '\w+' | sort |
uniq -c | sort -nr | head -n 10
```

The name shebang comes from the first two characters in the line: a hash (she) and an exclamation mark (bang). It's not a good idea to leave it out, as we have done in the previous step, because then the behavior of the script is undefined. The Bash shell, which is the one that we're using, uses the executable */bin/bash* by default. Other shells may have different defaults.

 Sometimes you will come across scripts that have a shebang in the form of `!/usr/bin/bash` or `!/usr/bin/python` (in the case of Python, as we will see in the next section). While this generally works, if the `bash` or `python` (Python Software Foundation, 2014) executables are installed in a different location than */usr/bin*, then the script does not work anymore. It's better to use the form presented here, namely `!/usr/bin/env bash` and `!/usr/bin/env python`, because the `env` (Mlynarik & MacKenzie, 2012) command-line tool is aware where `bash` and `python` are installed. In short, using `env` makes your scripts more portable.

Step 4: Remove Fixed Input

We now have a valid command-line tool that we can execute from the command line. But we can do better than this. We can make our command-line tool more reusable. The first command in our file is curl, which downloads the text from which we wish to obtain the top 10 most-used words. So the data and operations are combined into one.

But what if we wanted to obtain the top 10 most-used words from another ebook, or any other text for that matter? The input data is fixed within the tool itself. It would be better to separate the data from the command-line tool.

If we assume that the user of the command-line tool will provide the text, it will become more generally applicable. So, the solution is to simply remove the curl command from the script. See Example 4-3 for the updated script, named *top-words-4.sh*.

Example 4-3. ~/book/ch04/top-words-4.sh

```
#!/usr/bin/env bash
tr '[:upper:]' '[:lower:]' | grep -oE '\w+' | sort |
uniq -c | sort -nr | head -n 10
```

This works because if a script starts with a command that needs data from standard input, like tr, it will take the input that is given to the command-line tools. Assuming that we have saved the ebook to *data/finn.txt*, we could do, for example:

```
$ cat data/ | ./top-words-4.sh
```

 Although we haven't done so in our script, the same principle holds for saving data. It is, in general, better to let the user take care of that. Of course, if you intend to use a command-line tool only for your own projects, then there are no limits to how specific you can be.

Step 5: Parameterize

There is one more step that we can perform in order to make our command-line tool even more reusable: parameters. In our command-line tool, there are a number of fixed command-line arguments—for example, -nr for sort and -n 10 for head. It is probably best to keep the former argument fixed. However, it would be very useful to allow for different values for the head command. This would allow the end user to set the number of most-often used words to be outputted. Example 4-4 shows what our file *top-words-5.sh* looks like if we parameterize head.

Example 4-4. ~/book/ch04/top-words-5.sh

```
#!/usr/bin/env bash
NUM_WORDS="$1"                                              ❶
tr '[:upper:]' '[:lower:]' | grep -oE '\w+' | sort |
uniq -c | sort -nr | head -n $NUM_WORDS                     ❷
```

❶ The variable NUM_WORDS is set to the value of $1, which is a special variable in Bash. It holds the value of the first command-line argument passed to our command-line tool.

❷ Note that in order to use the value of the NUM_WORDS variable, you need to put a dollar sign ($) in front of it. When you set it, you do not write a dollar sign.

 We could use $1 directly as a value for the -n option to head and not bother creating an extra variable such as NUM_WORDS. However, with larger scripts and a few more command-line arguments such as $2 and $3, the code becomes more readable when you use named variables.

Now if we wanted to see the top 5 most-used words of our text, we would invoke our command-line tool as follows:

```
$ cat data/finn.txt | top-words-5.sh 5
```

If the user does not provide an argument, head will return an error message, because the value of *$1*, and therefore NUM_WORDS, will be an empty string.

```
$ cat data/finn.txt | top-words-5.sh
head: option requires an argument -- 'n'
Try 'head --help' for more information.
```

Step 6: Extend Your PATH

We're now finally finished building a reusable command-line tool. There is, however, one more step that can be very useful. This optional step ensures that you can execute your command-line tools from everywhere.

At the moment, when you want to execute your command-line tool, you either have to navigate to the directory it's in or include the full path name as shown in step 2. This is fine if the command-line tool is specifically built for, say, a certain project. However, if your command-line tool could be applied in multiple situations, then it's useful to be able to execute it from everywhere, just like the command-line tools that are already installed.

To accomplish this, Bash needs to know where to look for your command-line tools. It does this by traversing a list of directories that are stored in an environment variable called PATH. In a fresh install of the Data Science Toolbox, the PATH looks like this:

```
$ echo $PATH | fold
/usr/local/sbin:/usr/local/bin:/usr/sbin:/usr/bin:/sbin:/bin:/usr/games:/usr/loc
al/games:/home/vagrant/tools:/usr/lib/go/bin:/home/vagrant/.go/bin:/home/vagrant
/.data-science-at-the-command-line/tools:/home/vagrant/.bin
```

The directories are delimited by colons. Here is the list of directories:

```
$ echo $PATH | tr : '\n' | sort
/bin
/home/vagrant/.bin
/home/vagrant/.data-science-at-the-command-line/tools
/home/vagrant/.go/bin
/home/vagrant/tools
/sbin
/usr/bin
/usr/games
/usr/lib/go/bin
/usr/local/bin
/usr/local/games
/usr/local/sbin
/usr/sbin
```

To change the PATH permanently, you'll need to edit the *.bashrc* or *.profile* file located in your home directory. If you put all your custom command-line tools into one directory, say, *~/tools*, then you'll only need to change the PATH once. As you can see, the Data Science Toolbox already has */home/vagrant/.bin* in its PATH. Now, you no longer need to add the ./, but you can just use the filename. Moreover, you no longer need to remember where the command-line tool is, because you can use which to locate it.

Creating Command-Line Tools with Python and R

The command-line tool that we created in the previous section was written in Bash. (Sure, not every feature of the Bash language was employed, but the interpreter still was bash.) As you may know by now, the command line is language agnostic, so we do not necessarily have to use Bash for creating command-line tools.

In this section, we'll see that command-line tools can be created in other programming languages as well. We will focus on Python and R because these are currently the two most popular programming languages within the data science community. A complete introduction to these languages is outside the scope of this book, so we assume that you have some familiarity with Python and or R. Programming languages such as Java, Go, and Julia follow a similar pattern when it comes to creating command-line tools.

There are three main reasons for creating command-line tools in a programming language instead of Bash. First, you may have existing code that you wish to be able to use from the command line. Second, the command-line tool would end up encompassing more than a hundred lines of code. Third, the command-line tool needs to be very fast.

The six steps in the previous section roughly apply to creating command-line tools in other programming languages as well. The first step, however, would not be copying and pasting from the command line, but rather copying and pasting the relevant code into a new file. Command-line tools in Python and R need to specify python (Python Software Foundation, 2014) and Rscript (R Foundation for Statistical Computing, 2014), respectively, as the interpreter after the shebang.

When it comes to creating command-line tools using Python and R, there are two more aspects that deserve special attention, which will be discussed next. First, processing standard input, which comes natural to shell scripts, has to be taken care of explicitly in Python and R. Second, as command-line tools written in Python and R tend to be more complex, we may also want to offer the user the ability to specify more complex command-line arguments.

Porting the Shell Script

As a starting point, let's see how we would port the prior shell script to both Python and R. In other words, what Python and R code gives us the most often-used words from standard input? It is not important whether implementing this task in anything other than a shell programming language is a good idea. What matters is that it gives us a good opportunity to compare Bash with Python and R.

We will first show the two files *top-words.py* and *top-words.R* and then discuss the differences with the shell code. In Python, the code could would look something like Example 4-5.

Example 4-5. ~/book/ch04/top-words.py

```
#!/usr/bin/env python
import re
import sys
from collections import Counter
num_words = int(sys.argv[1])
text = sys.stdin.read().lower()
words = re.split('\W+', text)
cnt = Counter(words)
for word, count in cnt.most_common(num_words):
    print "%7d %s" % (count, word)
```

Example 4-5 uses pure Python. When you want to do advanced text processing, we recommend you check out the NLTK package (Perkins, 2010). If you are going to work with a lot of numerical data, then we recommend you use the Pandas package (McKinney, 2012).

And in R, the code would look something like Example 4-6 (thanks to Hadley Wickham):

Example 4-6. ~/book/ch04/top-words.R

```
#!/usr/bin/env Rscript
n <- as.integer(commandArgs(trailingOnly = TRUE))
f <- file("stdin")
lines <- readLines(f)
words <- tolower(unlist(strsplit(lines, "\\W+")))
counts <- sort(table(words), decreasing = TRUE)
counts_n <- counts[1:n]
cat(sprintf("%7d %s\n", counts_n, names(counts_n)), sep = "")
close(f)
```

Let's check that all three implementations (i.e., Bash, Python, and R) return the same top 5 words with the same counts:

```
$ < data/76.txt ./top-words-5.sh 5
   6441 and
   5082 the
   3666 i
   3258 a
   3022 to
$ < data/76.txt ./top-words.py 5
   6441 and
   5082 the
   3666 i
   3258 a
   3022 to
$ < data/76.txt ./top-words.R 5
   6441 and
   5082 the
   3666 i
   3258 a
   3022 to
```

Wonderful! Sure, the output itself is not very exciting. What *is* exciting is the observation that we can accomplish the same task with multiple approaches. Let's have a look at the differences between the approaches.

First, what's immediately obvious is the difference in amount of code. For this specific task, both Python and R require much more code than Bash. This illustrates that, for some tasks, it can be more efficient to use the command line. For other tasks, you may be better off using a programming language. As you gain more experience on the command-line, you will start to recognize when to use which approach. When everything is a command-line tool, you can even split up the task into subtasks, and combine a Bash command-line tool with, say, a Python command-line tool. Whichever approach works best for the task at hand!

Processing Streaming Data from Standard Input

In the previous two code examples, both Python and R read the complete standard input at once. On the command line, most command-line tools pipe data to the next command-line tool in a streaming fashion. (There are a few command-line tools that require the complete data before they write any data to standard output, like sort and awk (Brennan, 1994).) This means the pipeline is blocked by such command-line tools. This does not have to be a problem when the input data is finite, like a file. However, when the input data is a nonstop stream, such blocking command-line tools are useless.

Luckily, Python and R can both process data in a streaming matter. You can apply a function on a line-per-line basis, for example. Examples 4-7 and 4-8 are two minimal examples that demonstrate how this works in Python and R, respectively. They compute the square of every integer that is piped to them.

Example 4-7. ~/book/ch04/stream.py

```python
#!/usr/bin/env python
from sys import stdin, stdout
while True:
    line = stdin.readline()
    if not line:
        break
    stdout.write("%d\n" % int(line)**2)
    stdout.flush()
```

Example 4-8. ~/book/ch04/stream.R

```r
#!/usr/bin/env Rscript
f <- file("stdin")
open(f)
while(length(line <- readLines(f, n = 1)) > 0) {
        write(as.integer(line)^2, stdout())
}
close(f)
```

Further Reading

- Docopt. (2014). *Command-Line Interface Description Language*. Retrieved from *http://docopt.org*.

- Robbins, A., & Beebe, N. H. F. (2005). *Classic Shell Scripting*. O'Reilly Media.

- Peek, J., Powers, S., O'Reilly, T., & Loukides, M. (2002). *Unix Power Tools* (3rd Ed.). O'Reilly Media.

- Perkins, J. (2010). *Python Text Processing with NLTK 2.0 Cookbook*. Packt Publishing.

- McKinney, W. (2012). *Python for Data Analysis*. O'Reilly Media.

- Rossant, C. (2013). *Learning IPython for Interactive Computing and Data Visualization*. Packt Publishing.

- Wirzenius, L. (2013). Writing Manual Pages. Retrieved from *http://liw.fi/manpages/*.

- Raymond, E. S. (2014). Basics of the Unix Philosophy. Retrieved from *http://www.faqs.org/docs/artu/ch01s06.html*.

## CHAPTER 5

Scrubbing Data

In Chapter 2, we looked at the first step of the OSEMN model for data science, how to obtain data from a variety of sources. It's not uncommon for this data to have missing values, inconsistencies, errors, weird characters, or uninteresting columns. Sometimes we only need a specific portion of the data. And sometimes we need the data to be in a different format. In those cases, we have to clean, or *scrub*, the data before we can move on to the third step: exploring data.

The data we obtained in Chapter 3 can come in a variety of formats. The most common ones are plain text, CSV, JSON, and HTML/XML. Because most command-line tools operate on one format only, it is worthwhile to be able to convert data from one format to another.

CSV, which is the main format we're working with in this chapter, is actually not the easiest format to work with. Many CSV data sets are broken or incompatible with each other because there is no standard syntax, unlike XML and JSON.

Once our data is in the format we want it to be, we can apply common scrubbing operations. These include filtering, replacing, and merging data. The command line is especially well-suited for these kind of operations, as there exist many powerful command-line tools that are optimized for handling large amounts of data. Tools that we'll discuss in this chapter include classic ones such as: cut (Ihnat, MacKenzie, & Meyering, 2012) and sed (Fenlason, Lord, Pizzini, & Bonzini, 2012), and newer ones such as jq (Dolan, 2014) and csvgrep (Groskopf, 2014).

The scrubbing tasks that we discuss in this chapter not only apply to the input data. Sometimes, we also need to reformat the output of some command-line tools. For example, to transform the output of uniq -c to a CSV data set, we could use awk (Brennan, 1994) and header:

```
$ echo 'foo\nbar\nfoo' | sort | uniq -c | sort -nr
      2 foo
      1 bar
$ echo 'foo\nbar\nfoo' | sort | uniq -c | sort -nr |
> awk '{print $2","$1}' | header -a value,count
value,count
foo,2
bar,1
```

If your data requires additional functionality than what is offered by (a combination of) these command-line tools, you can use csvsql. This command-line tool allows you to perform SQL queries directly on CSV files. And remember, if after reading this chapter you still need more flexibility, you're free to use R, Python, or whatever programming language you prefer.

The command-line tools will be introduced on a need-to-use basis. You'll notice that sometimes we can use the same command-line tool to perform multiple operations, or vice versa, multiple command-line tools to perform the same operation. This chapter is more structured like a cookbook, where the focus is on the problems or recipes, rather than on the command-line tools.

Overview

In this chapter, you'll learn how to:

- Convert data from one format to another
- Apply SQL queries to CSV
- Filter lines
- Extract and replace values
- Split, merge, and extract columns

Common Scrub Operations for Plain Text

In this section we describe common scrubbing operations for plain text. Formally, plain text refers to a sequence of human-readable characters and optionally, some specific types of control characters (e.g., a tab or a newline; for more information, see: *http://www.linfo.org/plain_text.html*). Examples include: ebooks, emails, logfiles, and source code.

For the purpose of this book, we assume that the plain text contains some data, and that it has no clear tabular structure (like the CSV format) or nested structure (like the JSON and HTML/XML formats). We discuss those formats later in this chapter. Although these operations can also be applied to CSV, JSON, and HTML/XML formats, keep in mind that the tools treat the data as plain text.

Filtering Lines

The first scrubbing operation is filtering lines. This means that from the input data, each line will be evaluated to determine whether it may be passed on as output.

Based on location

The most straightforward way to filter lines is based on their location. This may be useful when you want to inspect, say, the top 10 lines of a file, or when you extract a specific row from the output of another command-line tool. To illustrate how to filter based on location, let's create a dummy file that contains 10 lines:

```
$ cd ~/book/ch05/data
$ seq -f "Line %g" 10 | tee lines
Line 1
Line 2
Line 3
Line 4
Line 5
Line 6
Line 7
Line 8
Line 9
Line 10
```

We can print the first three lines using either head, sed, or awk:

```
$ < lines head -n 3
$ < lines sed -n '1,3p'
$ < lines awk 'NR<=3'
Line 1
Line 2
Line 3
```

Similarly, we can print the last three lines using tail (Rubin, MacKenzie, Taylor, & Meyering, 2012):

```
$ < lines tail -n 3
Line 8
Line 9
Line 10
```

You can also you use sed and awk for this, but tail is much faster. Removing the first three lines goes as follows:

```
$ < lines tail -n +4
$ < lines sed '1,3d'
$ < lines sed -n '1,3!p'
Line 4
Line 5
Line 6
Line 7
```

```
Line 8
Line 9
Line 10
```

Notice that with `tail` you have to add one. Removing the last three lines can be done with `head`:

```
$ < lines head -n -3
Line 1
Line 2
Line 3
Line 4
Line 5
Line 6
Line 7
```

You can print (or extract) specific lines (4, 5, and 6 in this case) using either `sed`, `awk`, or a combination of `head` and `tail`:

```
$ < lines sed -n '4,6p'
$ < lines awk '(NR>=4)&&(NR<=6)'
$ < lines head -n 6 | tail -n 3
Line 4
Line 5
Line 6
```

Print odd numbered lines with `sed` by specifying a start and a step, or with `awk` by using the modulo operator:

```
$ < lines sed -n '1~2p'
$ < lines awk 'NR%2'
Line 1
Line 3
Line 5
Line 7
Line 9
```

Printing even numbered lines works in a similar manner:

```
$ < lines sed -n '0~2p'
$ < lines awk '(NR+1)%2'
Line 2
Line 4
Line 6
Line 8
Line 10
```

Based on pattern

Sometimes you want to extract or remove lines based on their contents. Using `grep`, the canonical command-line tool for filtering lines, we can print every line that matches a certain pattern or regular expression. For example, to extract all the chapter headings from *Alice's Adventures in Wonderland*:

```
$ grep -i chapter alice.txt
CHAPTER I. Down the Rabbit-Hole
CHAPTER II. The Pool of Tears
CHAPTER III. A Caucus-Race and a Long Tale
CHAPTER IV. The Rabbit Sends in a Little Bill
CHAPTER V. Advice from a Caterpillar
CHAPTER VI. Pig and Pepper
CHAPTER VII. A Mad Tea-Party
CHAPTER VIII. The Queen's Croquet-Ground
CHAPTER IX. The Mock Turtle's Story
CHAPTER X. The Lobster Quadrille
CHAPTER XI. Who Stole the Tarts?
CHAPTER XII. Alice's Evidence
```

Here, -i means case-insensitive. We can also specify a regular expression. For example, if we only wanted to print out the headings which start with "The":

```
$ grep -E '^CHAPTER (.*)\. The' alice.txt
CHAPTER II. The Pool of Tears
CHAPTER IV. The Rabbit Sends in a Little Bill
CHAPTER VIII. The Queen's Croquet-Ground
CHAPTER IX. The Mock Turtle's Story
CHAPTER X. The Lobster Quadrille
```

Note that you have to specify the -E option in order to enable regular expressions. Otherwise, grep interprets the pattern as a literal string.

Based on randomness

When you're in the process of formulating your data pipeline and you have a lot of data, then debugging your pipeline can be cumbersome. In that case, sampling from the data might be useful. The main purpose of the command-line tool sample (Janssens, 2014) is to get a subset of the data by outputting only a certain percentage of the input on a line-by-line basis:

```
$ seq 1000 | sample -r 1% | jq -c '{line: .}'
{"line":53}
{"line":119}
{"line":141}
{"line":228}
{"line":464}
{"line":476}
{"line":523}
{"line":657}
{"line":675}
{"line":865}
{"line":948}
```

Here, every input line has a 1% chance of being forwarded to jq. This percentage could also have been specified as a fraction (1/100) or as a probability (0.01).

sample has two other purposes, which can be useful when you're in debugging mode. First, it's possible to add some delay to the output. This comes in handy when the input is a constant stream (e.g., the Twitter firehose), and the data comes in too fast to see what's going on. Secondly, you can put a timer on sample. This way, you don't have to kill the ongoing process manually. To add a 1-second delay between each output line to the previous command and to only run for 5 seconds:

```
$ seq 10000 | sample -r 1% -d 1000 -s 5 | jq -c '{line: .}'
```

In order to prevent unnecessary computation, try to put sample as early as possible in your pipeline (this advice holds for any command-line tool that reduces data, like head and tail). Once you're done debugging, you can simply take it out of the pipeline.

Extracting Values

To extract the actual chapter headings from our example earlier, we can take a simple approach by piping the output of grep to cut:

```
$ grep -i chapter alice.txt | cut -d' ' -f3-
Down the Rabbit-Hole
The Pool of Tears
A Caucus-Race and a Long Tale
The Rabbit Sends in a Little Bill
Advice from a Caterpillar
Pig and Pepper
A Mad Tea-Party
The Queen's Croquet-Ground
The Mock Turtle's Story
The Lobster Quadrille
Who Stole the Tarts?
Alice's Evidence
```

Here, each line that's passed to cut is split on spaces into fields, and then the third field to the last field is being printed. The total number of fields can be different per input line. With sed, we can accomplish the same task in a much more complex manner:

```
$ sed -rn 's/^CHAPTER ([IVXLCDM]{1,})\. (.*)$/\2/p' alice.txt > /dev/null
```

(Because the output is the same it's omitted by redirecting it to */dev/null*.) This approach uses a regular expression and a back reference. Here, sed also takes over the work done by grep. This complex approach is only advisable when a simpler one would not work. For example, if "chapter" was ever part of the text itself and not just used to indicate the start of a new chapter. Of course there are many levels of complexity which would have worked around this, but this was to illustrate an extremely strict approach. In practice, the challenge is to find a good balance between complexity and flexibility.

It's worth noting that cut can also split on character positions. This is useful for when you want to extract (or remove) the same set of characters per input line:

```
$ grep -i chapter alice.txt | cut -c 9-
I. Down the Rabbit-Hole
II. The Pool of Tears
III. A Caucus-Race and a Long Tale
IV. The Rabbit Sends in a Little Bill
V. Advice from a Caterpillar
VI. Pig and Pepper
VII. A Mad Tea-Party
VIII. The Queen's Croquet-Ground
IX. The Mock Turtle's Story
X. The Lobster Quadrille
XI. Who Stole the Tarts?
XII. Alice's Evidence
```

grep has a great feature that outputs every match onto a separate line:

```
$ < alice.txt grep -oE '\w{2,}' | head
Project
Gutenberg
Alice
Adventures
in
Wonderland
by
Lewis
Carroll
This
```

But what if we wanted to create a data set of all the words that start with an "a" and end with an "e". Well, of course there's a pipeline for that, too:

```
$ < alice.txt tr '[:upper:]' '[:lower:]' | grep -oE '\w{2,}' |
> grep -E '^a.*e$' | sort | uniq -c | sort -nr |
> awk '{print $2","$1}' | header -a word,count | head | csvlook
|-------------+-------|
| word        | count |
|-------------+-------|
| alice       | 403   |
| are         | 73    |
| archive     | 13    |
| agree       | 11    |
| anyone      | 5     |
| alone       | 5     |
| age         | 4     |
| applicable  | 3     |
| anywhere    | 3     |
| alive       | 3     |
|-------------+-------|
```

Replacing and Deleting Values

You can use the command-line tool tr, which stands for *translate*, to replace individual characters. For example, spaces can be replaced by underscores as follows:

```
$ echo 'hello world!' | tr ' ' '_'
hello_world!
```

If more than one character needs to be replaced, then you can combine that:

```
$ echo 'hello world!' | tr ' !' '_?'
hello_world?
```

tr can also be used to delete individual characters by specifying the -d option:

```
$ echo 'hello world!' | tr -d -c '[a-z]'
helloworld
```

Here, we've actually used two more features. First, we've specified a set of characters (all lowercase letters). Second, we've indicated with the -c option that the complement should be used. In other words, this command only retains lowercase letters. We can even use tr to convert our text to uppercase:

```
$ echo 'hello world!' | tr '[a-z]' '[A-Z]'
HELLO WORLD!
$ echo 'hello world!' | tr '[:lower:]' '[:upper:]'
HELLO WORLD!
```

The latter command is preferable because that also handles non-ASCII characters. If you need to operate on more than individual characters, then you may find sed useful. We've already seen an example of sed with extracting the chapter headings from *Alice in Wonderland*. Extracting, deleting, and replacing is actually all the same operation in sed. You just specify different regular expressions. For example, to change a word, remove repeated spaces, and remove leading spaces:

```
$ echo ' hello     world!' | sed -re 's/hello/bye/;s/\s+/ /g;s/\s+//'
bye world!
```

The g flag stands for *global*, meaning that the same part can be applied more than once on the same line. We do not need that with the second part, which removes leading spaces. Note that regular expressions of the first and the last parts could have been combined into one regular expression.

Working with CSV

Bodies and Headers and Columns, Oh My!

The command-line tools that we've used to scrub plain text, such as tr and grep, cannot always be applied to CSV. The reason is that these command-line tools have no notion of headers, bodies, and columns. What if we wanted to filter lines using grep but always include the header in the output? Or what if we only wanted to uppercase the values of a specific column using tr and leave the other columns untouched? There are multistep workarounds for this, but they're very cumbersome. We have something better. In order to leverage ordinary command-line tools for CSV, we'd like to introduce you to three command-line tools, aptly named: body (Janssens, 2014), header (Janssens, 2014), and cols (Janssens, 2014).

Let's start with the first command-line tool: body. With body, you can apply any command-line tool to the body of a CSV file (i.e., everything excluding the header). For example:

```
$ echo -e "value\n7\n2\n5\n3" | body sort -n
value
2
3
5
7
```

It assumes that the header of the CSV file only spans one row. Here's the source code for completeness:

```
#!/usr/bin/env bash
IFS= read -r header        ❶
printf '%s\n' "$header"    ❷
$@                         ❸
```

It works like this:

❶   Take one line from standard input and store it as a variable named *$header*.

❷   Print out the header.

❸   Execute all the command-line arguments passed to body on the remaining data.

Here's another example. Imagine that we count the lines of the following CSV file:

```
$ seq 5 | header -a count
count
1
2
3
4
5
```

With wc -l, we can count the number of all lines:

```
$ seq 5 | header -a count | wc -l
6
```

If we only want to consider the lines in the body (so everything except the header), we simply add body:

```
$ seq 5 | header -a count | body wc -l
count
5
```

Note that the header is not used, and is also printed again in the output.

The second command-line tool, header, allows us, as the name implies, to manipulate the header of a CSV file. The complete source code is as follows:

```
#!/usr/bin/env bash
get_header () {
        for i in $(seq $NUMROWS); do
                IFS= read -r LINE
                OLDHEADER="${OLDHEADER}${LINE}\n"
        done
}

print_header () {
        echo -ne "$1"
}

print_body () {
        cat
}

OLDHEADER=
NUMROWS=1

while getopts "dn:ha:r:e:" OPTION
do
        case $OPTION in
                n)
                        NUMROWS=$OPTARG
                        ;;
                a)
                        print_header "$OPTARG\n"
                        print_body
                        exit 1
                        ;;
                d)
                        get_header
                        print_body
                        exit 1
                        ;;
                r)
                        get_header
                        print_header "$OPTARG\n"
                        print_body
                        exit 1
                        ;;
                e)
                        get_header
                        print_header "$(echo -ne $OLDHEADER | eval $OPTARG)\n"
```

```
                              print_body
                              exit 1
                              ;;
                     h)
                              usage
                              exit 1
                              ;;
              esac
       done

       get_header
       print_header $OLDHEADER
```

If no arguments are provided, the header of the CSV file is printed:

```
$ < tips.csv header
bill,tip,sex,smoker,day,time,size
```

This is the same as head -n 1. If the header spans more than one row, which is generally not recommended, you can specify -n 2. We can also add a header to a CSV file:

```
$ seq 5 | header -a count
count
1
2
3
4
5
```

This is equivalent to echo "count" | cat - <(seq 5). Deleting a header is done with the -d option:

```
$ < iris.csv header -d | head
5.1,3.5,1.4,0.2,Iris-setosa
4.9,3.0,1.4,0.2,Iris-setosa
4.7,3.2,1.3,0.2,Iris-setosa
4.6,3.1,1.5,0.2,Iris-setosa
5.0,3.6,1.4,0.2,Iris-setosa
5.4,3.9,1.7,0.4,Iris-setosa
4.6,3.4,1.4,0.3,Iris-setosa
5.0,3.4,1.5,0.2,Iris-setosa
4.4,2.9,1.4,0.2,Iris-setosa
4.9,3.1,1.5,0.1,Iris-setosa
```

This is similar to tail -n +2, but it's a bit easier to remember. Replacing a header, which is basically first deleting a header and then adding one if you look at the preceding source code, is accomplished with specifying -r. Here, we combine it with body:

```
$ seq 5 | header -a line | body wc -l | header -r count
count
5
```

And last but not least, we can apply a command to just the header, similar to what the body command-line tool does to the body:

```
$ seq 5 | header -a line | header -e "tr '[a-z]' '[A-Z]'"
LINE
1
2
3
4
5
```

The third command-line tool is called `cols`, which is similar to `header` and body in that it allows you to apply a certain command to only a subset of the columns. The code is as follows:

```
#!/usr/bin/env bash
ARG="$1"
shift
COLUMNS="$1"
shift
EXPR="$@"
DIRTMP=$(mktemp -d)
mkfifo $DIRTMP/other_columns
tee $DIRTMP/other_columns | csvcut $ARG $COLUMNS | ${EXPR} |
paste -d, - <(csvcut ${ARG~~} $COLUMNS $DIRTMP/other_columns)
rm -rf $DIRTMP
```

For example, if we wanted to uppercase the values in the day column in the *tips.csv* data set (without affecting the other columns and the header), we would use `cols` in combination with body, as follows:

```
$ < tips.csv cols -c day body "tr '[a-z]' '[A-Z]'" | head -n 5 | csvlook
|------+-------+------+--------+--------+--------+-------|
| day  | bill  | tip  | sex    | smoker | time   | size  |
|------+-------+------+--------+--------+--------+-------|
| SUN  | 16.99 | 1.01 | Female | No     | Dinner | 2     |
| SUN  | 10.34 | 1.66 | Male   | No     | Dinner | 3     |
| SUN  | 21.01 | 3.5  | Male   | No     | Dinner | 3     |
| SUN  | 23.68 | 3.31 | Male   | No     | Dinner | 2     |
|------+-------+------+--------+--------+--------+-------|
```

Note that passing multiple command-line tools and arguments as commands to header -e, body, and cols can lead to tricky quoting situations. If you ever run into such problems, it is best to create a separate command-line tool for this and pass that as the command.

In conclusion, while it is generally preferable to use command-line tools that are specifically made for CSV data, body, header, and cols also allow you to apply the classic command-line tools to CSV files if needed.

Performing SQL Queries on CSV

In case the command-line tools mentioned in this chapter do not provide enough flexibility, then there's another approach to scrub your data using the command line. The command-line tool `csvsql` (Groskopf, 2014) allows you to execute SQL queries directly on CSV files. As you may know, SQL is a very powerful language to define operations for scrubbing data; it's also a very different way than using individual command-line tools.

 If your data originally comes from a relational database, then, if possible, try to execute SQL queries on that database and subsequently extract the data as CSV. As discussed in Chapter 3, you can use the command-line tool `sql2csv` for this. When you first export data from the database to a CSV file, and then apply SQL, it is not only slower, but there is also a possibility that the column types are not correctly inferred from the CSV data.

In the scrubbing tasks below, we'll include several solutions that involve `csvsql`. The basic command is this:

```
$ seq 5 | header -a value | csvsql --query "SELECT SUM(value) AS sum FROM stdin"
sum
15
```

If you pass standard input to `csvsql`, then the table is named *stdin*. The types of the column are automatically inferred from the data. As you'll see later, in the combining CSV files section, you can also specify multiple CSV files. Keep in mind that `csvsql` employs the SQLite dialect. While SQL is generally more verbose than the other solutions, it's also much more flexible. If you already know how to tackle a scrubbing problem with SQL, then there's no shame in using it from the command line!

Working with HTML/XML and JSON

As we saw in Chapter 3, our obtained data can come in a variety of formats. The most common ones are plain text, CSV, JSON, and HTML/XML. In this section, we're going to demonstrate a couple of command-line tools that can convert our data from one format to another. There are two reasons to convert data.

First, oftentimes the data needs to be in tabular form, just like a database table or a spreadsheet, because many visualization and machine-learning algorithms depend on it. CSV is inherently in tabular form, but JSON and HTML/XML data can have a deeply nested structure.

Second, many command-line tools, especially the classic ones such as `cut` and `grep`, operate on plain text. This is because text is regarded as a universal interface between command-line tools. Moreover, the other formats are simply younger. Each of these formats can be treated as plain text, allowing us to apply such command-line tools to the other formats as well.

Sometimes we can get away with applying the classic tools to structured data. For example, by treating the JSON data as plain text, we can change the attribute "gender" to "sex" using sed:

```
$ sed -e 's/"gender":/"sex":/g' data/users.json | fold | head -n 3
{"results":[{"user":{"sex":"female","name":{"title":"mrs","first":"kaylee","last
":"anderson"},"location":{"street":"1779 washington ave","city":"cupertino","sta
te":"michigan","zip":"13931"},"email":"kaylee.anderson64@example.com","password"
```

Like many other command-line tools, sed does not make use of the structure of the data. Because of this, it's better to use a command-line tool that makes use of the structure of the data (as we will do with jq), or first convert the data to a tabular format such as CSV and then apply the appropriate command-line tool.

Next, we're going to demonstrate converting HTML/XML and JSON to CSV through a real-world use case. The command-line tools that we'll be using here are: curl, scrape (Janssens, 2014), xml2json (Parmentier, 2014), jq (Dolan, 2014), and json2csv (Czebotar, 2014).

Wikipedia holds a wealth of information. Much of this information is ordered in tables, which can be regarded as data sets. For example, the page *http://en.wikipe dia.org/wiki/List_of_countries_and_territories_by_border/area_ratio* contains a list of countries and territories together with their border length, their area, and the ratio between the two. Let's imagine that we're interested in analyzing this data set. In this section, we'll walk you through all the necessary steps and their corresponding commands.

The data set that we're interested in is embedded in HTML. Our goal is to end up with a representation of this data set that we can work with. The very first step is to download the HTML using curl:

```
$ curl -sL 'http://en.wikipedia.org/wiki/List_of_countries_and_territories_'\
> 'by_border/area_ratio' > wiki.html
```

The option -s causes curl to be silent and not output any other information but the actual HTML. The HTML is saved to a file named *data/wiki.html*. Here's what the first 10 lines look like:

```
$ head -n 10 data/wiki.html | cut -c1-79
<!DOCTYPE html>
<html lang="en" dir="ltr" class="client-nojs">
<head>
<meta charset="UTF-8" /><title>List of countries and territories by border/area
<meta http-equiv="X-UA-Compatible" content="IE=EDGE" /><meta name="generator" c
<link rel="alternate" type="application/x-wiki" title="Edit this page" href="/w
```

```
<link rel="edit" title="Edit this page" href="/w/index.php?title=List_of_countr
<link rel="apple-touch-icon" href="//bits.wikimedia.org/apple-touch/wikipedia.p
<link rel="shortcut icon" href="//bits.wikimedia.org/favicon/wikipedia.ico" />
<link rel="search" type="application/opensearchdescription+xml" href="/w/opense
```

That seems to be in order. (Note that we're only showing the first 79 characters of each line so that output fits on the page.)

Using the developer tools of our browser, we were able to determine that the root HTML element that we're interested in is a `<table>` with the class `wikitable`. This allows us to look at the part that we're interested in using `grep` (the `-A` option below specifies the number of lines we want to see after the matching line):

```
$ < wiki.html grep wikitable -A 21
<table class="wikitable sortable">
<tr>
<th>Rank</th>
<th>Country or territory</th>
<th>Total length of land borders (km)</th>
<th>Total surface area (km²)</th>
<th>Border/area ratio (km/km²)</th>
</tr>
<tr>
<td>1</td>
<td>Vatican City</td>
<td>3.2</td>
<td>0.44</td>
<td>7.2727273</td>
</tr>
<tr>
<td>2</td>
<td>Monaco</td>
<td>4.4</td>
<td>2</td>
<td>2.2000000</td>
</tr>
```

The next step is to extract the necessary elements from the HTML file. For this we use the `scrape` tool:

```
$ < wiki.html scrape -b -e 'table.wikitable > tr:not(:first-child)' \
> > table.html
$ head -n 21 data/table.html
<!DOCTYPE html>
<html>
<body>
<tr><td>1</td>
<td>Vatican City</td>
<td>3.2</td>
<td>0.44</td>
<td>7.2727273</td>
</tr>
```

```
<tr><td>2</td>
<td>Monaco</td>
<td>4.4</td>
<td>2</td>
<td>2.2000000</td>
</tr>
<tr><td>3</td>
<td>San Marino</td>
<td>39</td>
<td>61</td>
<td>0.6393443</td>
</tr>
```

The value passed to the -e option, which stands for *expression*, is a so-called CSS selector. The syntax is usually used to style web pages, but we can also use it to select certain elements from our HTML. In this case, we wish to select all <tr> elements or *rows* (except the first) that are part of a table which belongs to the wikitable class. This is precisely the table that we're interested in. The reason that we don't want the first row (specified by :not(first-child)) is that we don't want the header of the table. This results in a data set where each row represents a country or territory. As you can see, we now have the <tr> elements that we're looking for, encapsulated in <html> and <body> elements (because we specified the -b option). This ensures that our next tool, xml2json, can work with it.

As its name implies, xml2json converts XML (and HTML) to JSON.

```
$ < table.html xml2json > table.json
$ < table.json jq '.' | head -n 25
{
  "html": {
    "body": {
      "tr": [
        {
          "td": [
            {
              "$t": "1"
            },
            {
              "$t": "Vatican City"
            },
            {
              "$t": "3.2"
            },
            {
              "$t": "0.44"
            },
            {
              "$t": "7.2727273"
            }
          ]
        },
```

```
{
    "td": [
```

The reason we convert the HTML to JSON is because there is a very powerful tool called jq that operates on JSON data. The following command extracts certain parts of the JSON data and reshapes it into a form that we can work with:

```
$ < data/table.json jq -c '.html.body.tr[] | {country: .td[1][],border:'\
> '.td[2][], surface: .td[3][]}' > countries.json
$ head -n 10 data/countries.json
{"surface":"0.44","border":"3.2","country":"Vatican City"}
{"surface":"2","border":"4.4","country":"Monaco"}
{"surface":"61","border":"39","country":"San Marino"}
{"surface":"160","border":"76","country":"Liechtenstein"}
{"surface":"34","border":"10.2","country":"Sint Maarten (Netherlands)"}
{"surface":"468","border":"120.3","country":"Andorra"}
{"surface":"6","border":"1.2","country":"Gibraltar (United Kingdom)"}
{"surface":"54","border":"10.2","country":"Saint Martin (France)"}
{"surface":"2586","border":"359","country":"Luxembourg"}
{"surface":"6220","border":"466","country":"Palestinian territories"}
```

Now we're getting somewhere. JSON is a very popular data format with many advantages, but for our purposes we're better off having the data in CSV format. The tool json2csv is able to convert the data from JSON to CSV:

```
$ < countries.json json2csv -p -k border,surface > countries.csv
$ head -n 11 countries.csv | csvlook
|---------+---------|
| border  | surface |
|---------+---------|
| 3.2     | 0.44    |
| 4.4     | 2       |
| 39      | 61      |
| 76      | 160     |
| 10.2    | 34      |
| 120.3   | 468     |
| 1.2     | 6       |
| 10.2    | 54      |
| 359     | 2586    |
| 466     | 6220    |
|---------+---------|
```

The data is now in a form that we can work with. Those were quite a few steps to get from a Wikipedia page to a CSV data set. However, when you combine all of these commands into one, you will see that it's actually really concise and expressive:

```
$ curl -sL 'http://en.wikipedia.org/wiki/List_of_countries'\
> '_and_territories_by_border/area_ratio' |
> scrape -be 'table.wikitable > tr:not(:first-child)' |
> xml2json | jq -c '.html.body.tr[] | {country: .td[1][],'\
> 'border: .td[2][], surface: .td[3][], ratio: .td[4][]}' |
> json2csv -p -k=border,surface | head -n 11 | csvlook
|---------+---------|
```

```
| border | surface |
|---------+---------|
| 3.2    | 0.44    |
| 4.4    | 2       |
| 39     | 61      |
| 76     | 160     |
| 10.2   | 34      |
| 120.3  | 468     |
| 1.2    | 6       |
| 10.2   | 54      |
| 359    | 2586    |
| 466    | 6220    |
|---------+---------|
```

That concludes the demonstration of converting HTML/XML to JSON to CSV. Although jq can perform many more operations, and despite the specialized tools available for working with XML data, in our experience, converting the data to CSV format as quickly as possible tends to work well. This way you can spend more time becoming proficient at generic command-line tools, rather than very specific tools.

Common Scrub Operations for CSV

Extracting and Reordering Columns

Columns can be extracted and reordered using the command-line tool csvcut (Groskopf, 2014). For example, to keep only the columns in the Iris data set that contain numerical values *and* reorder the middle two columns:

```
$ < iris.csv csvcut -c sepal_length,petal_length,sepal_width,petal_width |
> head -n 5 | csvlook
|--------------+--------------+-------------+-------------|
| sepal_length | petal_length | sepal_width | petal_width |
|--------------+--------------+-------------+-------------|
| 5.1          | 1.4          | 3.5         | 0.2         |
| 4.9          | 1.4          | 3.0         | 0.2         |
| 4.7          | 1.3          | 3.2         | 0.2         |
| 4.6          | 1.5          | 3.1         | 0.2         |
|--------------+--------------+-------------+-------------|
```

Alternatively, we can also specify the columns we want to leave out with -C, which stands for *complement*:

```
$ < iris.csv csvcut -C species | head -n 5 | csvlook
|--------------+--------------+--------------+-------------|
| sepal_length | sepal_width  | petal_length | petal_width |
|--------------+--------------+--------------+-------------|
| 5.1          | 3.5          | 1.4          | 0.2         |
| 4.9          | 3.0          | 1.4          | 0.2         |
| 4.7          | 3.2          | 1.3          | 0.2         |
```

```
| 4.6          | 3.1          | 1.5          | 0.2          |
|--------------+--------------+--------------+--------------|
```

Here, the included columns are kept in the same order. Instead of the column names, you can also specify the indices of the columns, which start at 1. This allows you to, for example, select only the odd columns (should you ever need it!):

```
$ echo 'a,b,c,d,e,f,g,h,i\n1,2,3,4,5,6,7,8,9' |
> csvcut -c $(seq 1 2 9 | paste -sd,)
a,c,e,g,i
1,3,5,7,9
```

If you're certain that there are no commas in any of the values, then you can also use cut to extract columns. Be aware that cut does not reorder columns, as is demonstrated with the following command:

```
$ echo 'a,b,c,d,e,f,g,h,i\n1,2,3,4,5,6,7,8,9' | cut -d, -f 5,1,3
a,c,e
1,3,5
```

As you can see, it doesn't matter in which order we specify the columns; with cut they will always appear in the original order. For completeness, let's also take a look at the SQL approach for extracting and reordering the numerical columns of the Iris data set:

```
$ < iris.csv csvsql --query "SELECT sepal_length, petal_length, "\
> "sepal_width, petal_width FROM stdin" | head -n 5 | csvlook
|--------------+--------------+--------------+--------------|
|  sepal_length | petal_length | sepal_width | petal_width |
|--------------+--------------+--------------+--------------|
|  5.1          | 1.4          | 3.5          | 0.2          |
|  4.9          | 1.4          | 3.0          | 0.2          |
|  4.7          | 1.3          | 3.2          | 0.2          |
|  4.6          | 1.5          | 3.1          | 0.2          |
|--------------+--------------+--------------+--------------|
```

Filtering Lines

The difference between filtering lines in a CSV file as opposed to a plain-text file is that you may want to base this filtering on values in a certain column only. Filtering on location is essentially the same, but you have to take into account that the first line of a CSV file is usually the header. Remember that you can always use the body command-line tool if you want to keep the header:

```
$ seq 5 | sed -n '3,5p'
3
4
5
$ seq 5 | header -a count | body sed -n '3,5p'
count
3
```

When it comes down to filtering on a certain pattern within a certain column, we can use either `csvgrep`, `awk`, or, of course, `csvsql`. For example, to exclude all the bills of which the party size was 4 or less:

```
$ csvgrep -c size -i -r "[1-4]" tips.csv | csvlook
|--------+------+--------+--------+------+--------+-------|
| bill   | tip  | sex    | smoker | day  | time   | size  |
|--------+------+--------+--------+------+--------+-------|
| 29.8   | 4.2  | Female | No     | Thur | Lunch  | 6     |
| 34.3   | 6.7  | Male   | No     | Thur | Lunch  | 6     |
| 41.19  | 5.0  | Male   | No     | Thur | Lunch  | 5     |
| 27.05  | 5.0  | Female | No     | Thur | Lunch  | 6     |
| 29.85  | 5.14 | Female | No     | Sun  | Dinner | 5     |
| 48.17  | 5.0  | Male   | No     | Sun  | Dinner | 6     |
| 20.69  | 5.0  | Male   | No     | Sun  | Dinner | 5     |
| 30.46  | 2.0  | Male   | Yes    | Sun  | Dinner | 5     |
| 28.15  | 3.0  | Male   | Yes    | Sat  | Dinner | 5     |
|--------+------+--------+--------+------+--------+-------|
```

Both `awk` and `csvsql` can also do numerical comparisons. For example, to get all the bills above 40 USD on a Saturday or a Sunday:

```
$ < tips.csv awk -F, '($1 > 40.0) && ($5 ~ /S/)' | csvlook
|--------+------+--------+-----+-----+--------+----|
| 48.27  | 6.73 | Male   | No  | Sat | Dinner | 4  |
|--------+------+--------+-----+-----+--------+----|
| 44.3   | 2.5  | Female | Yes | Sat | Dinner | 3  |
| 48.17  | 5.0  | Male   | No  | Sun | Dinner | 6  |
| 50.81  | 10.0 | Male   | Yes | Sat | Dinner | 3  |
| 45.35  | 3.5  | Male   | Yes | Sun | Dinner | 3  |
| 40.55  | 3.0  | Male   | Yes | Sun | Dinner | 2  |
| 48.33  | 9.0  | Male   | No  | Sat | Dinner | 4  |
|--------+------+--------+-----+-----+--------+----|
```

The `csvsql` solution is more verbose but is also more robust, as it uses the names of the columns instead of their indexes:

```
$ < tips.csv csvsql --query "SELECT * FROM stdin "\
> "WHERE bill > 40 AND day LIKE '%S%'" | csvlook
|--------+------+--------+--------+-----+--------+-------|
| bill   | tip  | sex    | smoker | day | time   | size  |
|--------+------+--------+--------+-----+--------+-------|
| 48.27  | 6.73 | Male   | 0      | Sat | Dinner | 4     |
| 44.3   | 2.5  | Female | 1      | Sat | Dinner | 3     |
| 48.17  | 5.0  | Male   | 0      | Sun | Dinner | 6     |
| 50.81  | 10.0 | Male   | 1      | Sat | Dinner | 3     |
| 45.35  | 3.5  | Male   | 1      | Sun | Dinner | 3     |
| 40.55  | 3.0  | Male   | 1      | Sun | Dinner | 2     |
| 48.33  | 9.0  | Male   | 0      | Sat | Dinner | 4     |
|--------+------+--------+--------+-----+--------+-------|
```

It should be noted that the flexibility of the WHERE clause in an SQL query cannot be easily matched with other command-line tools, as SQL can operate on dates and sets and form complex combinations of clauses.

Merging Columns

Merging columns is useful for when the values of interest are spread over multiple columns. This may happen with dates (where year, month, and day could be separate columns) or names (where the first name and last name are separate columns). Let's consider the second situation.

The input CSV is a list of contemporary composers. Imagine our task is to combine the first name and the last name into a full name. We'll present four different approaches for this task: sed, awk, cols/tr, and csvsql. Let's have a look at the input CSV:

```
$ < names.csv csvlook
|------+-----------+-------------+------|
|  id  | last_name | first_name  | born |
|------+-----------+-------------+------|
|  1   | Williams  | John        | 1932 |
|  2   | Elfman    | Danny       | 1953 |
|  3   | Horner    | James       | 1953 |
|  4   | Shore     | Howard      | 1946 |
|  5   | Zimmer    | Hans        | 1957 |
|------+-----------+-------------+------|
```

The first approach, sed, uses an expression with two parts. The first part is to replace the header and the second part is a regular expression with back references applied to the second row onwards:

```
$ < names.csv sed -re '1s/.*/id,full_name,born/g;'\
> '2,$s/(.*),(.*),(.*),(.*)/\1,\3 \2,\4/g' | csvlook
|------+----------------+------|
|  id  | full_name      | born |
|------+----------------+------|
|  1   | John Williams  | 1932 |
|  2   | Danny Elfman   | 1953 |
|  3   | James Horner   | 1953 |
|  4   | Howard Shore   | 1946 |
|  5   | Hans Zimmer    | 1957 |
|------+----------------+------|
```

The awk approach looks as follows:

```
$ < names.csv awk -F, 'BEGIN{OFS=","; print "id,full_name,born"}'\
> '{if(NR > 1) {print $1,$3" "$2,$4}}' | csvlook
|------+----------------+------|
|  id  | full_name      | born |
|------+----------------+------|
|  1   | John Williams  | 1932 |
```

```
|   2  | Danny Elfman  | 1953  |
|   3  | James Horner  | 1953  |
|   4  | Howard Shore  | 1946  |
|   5  | Hans Zimmer   | 1957  |
|-----+---------------+-------|
```

The `cols` approach in combination with `tr`:

```
$ < names.csv cols -c first_name,last_name tr \",\" \" \" |
> header -r full_name,id,born | csvcut -c id,full_name,born | csvlook
|-----+---------------+-------|
| id  | full_name     | born  |
|-----+---------------+-------|
|  1  | John Williams | 1932  |
|  2  | Danny Elfman  | 1953  |
|  3  | James Horner  | 1953  |
|  4  | Howard Shore  | 1946  |
|  5  | Hans Zimmer   | 1957  |
|-----+---------------+-------|
```

Note that `csvsql` employs SQLite as the database to execute the query and that `||` stands for concatenation:

```
$ < names.csv csvsql --query "SELECT id, first_name || ' ' || last_name "\
> "AS full_name, born FROM stdin" | csvlook
|-----+-----------------------+-------|
| id  | full_name             | born  |
|-----+-----------------------+-------|
|  1  | John Williams         | 1932  |
|  2  | Danny Elfman          | 1953  |
|  3  | James Horner          | 1953  |
|  4  | Howard Shore          | 1946  |
|  5  | Hans Zimmer           | 1957  |
|-----+-----------------------+-------|
```

What if `last_name` contained a comma? Let's have a look at the raw input CSV for clarity's sake:

```
$ cat names-comma.csv
id,last_name,first_name,born
1,Williams,John,1932
2,Elfman,Danny,1953
3,Horner,James,1953
4,Shore,Howard,1946
5,Zimmer,Hans,1957
6,"Beethoven, van",Ludwig,1770
```

Well, it appears that the first three approaches fail; all in different ways. Only `csvsql` is able to combine `first_name` and `full_name` properly:

```
$ < names-comma.csv sed -re '1s/.*/id,full_name,born/g;'\
> '2,$s/(.*),(.*),(.*),(.*)/\1,\3 \2,\4/g' | tail -n 1
6,"Beethoven,Ludwig  van",1770
```

```
$ < names-comma.csv awk -F, 'BEGIN{OFS=","; print "id,full_name,born"}'\
> '{if(NR > 1) {print $1,$3" "$2,$4}}' | tail -n 1
6, van" "Beethoven,Ludwig

$ < names-comma.csv cols -c first_name,last_name tr \",\" \" \" |
> header -r full_name,id,born | csvcut -c id,full_name,born | tail -n 1
6,"Ludwig ""Beethoven  van""",1770

$ < names-comma.csv csvsql --query "SELECT id, first_name || ' ' || last_name\
> " AS full_name, born FROM stdin" | tail -n 1
6,"Ludwig Beethoven, van",1770

$ < names-comma.csv Rio -e 'df$full_name <- paste(df$first_name,df$last_name);'\
> 'df[c("id","full_name","born")]' | tail -n 1
6,"Ludwig Beethoven, van",1770
```

Wait a minute! What's that last command? Is that R? Well, as a matter of fact, it is. It's R code evaluated through a command-line tool called Rio (Janssens, 2014). All that we can say at this moment is that this approach also succeeds at merging the two columns. We'll discuss this nifty command-line tool later.

Combining Multiple CSV Files

Concatenate vertically

Vertical concatenation may be necessary in cases where you have, for example, a data set that is generated on a daily basis, or where each data set represents a different market or product. Let's simulate the latter by splitting up our beloved Iris data set into three CSV files, so that we have something to combine again. We'll use fields plit (Hinds et al., 2010), which is part of the CRUSH suite of command-line tools:

```
$ < iris.csv fieldsplit -d, -k -F species -p . -s .csv
```

Here, the options specify: the delimiter (-d), that we want to keep the header in each file (-k), the column whose values dictate the possible output files (-F), the relative output path (-p), and the filename suffix (-s), respectively. Because the species column in the Iris data set contains three different values, we end up with three CSV files, each with 50 lines and a header:

```
$ wc -l Iris-*.csv
  51 Iris-setosa.csv
  51 Iris-versicolor.csv
  51 Iris-virginica.csv
 153 total
```

You could just concatenate the files back using cat and removing the headers of all but the first file using header -d as follows:

```
$ cat Iris-setosa.csv <(< Iris-versicolor.csv header -d) \
> <(< Iris-virginica.csv header -d) | sed -n '1p;49,54p' | csvlook
|---------------+-------------+-------------+-------------+-----------------|
```

```
| sepal_length | sepal_width | petal_length | petal_width | species          |
|--------------+-------------+--------------+-------------+------------------|
| 4.6          | 3.2         | 1.4          | 0.2         | Iris-setosa      |
| 5.3          | 3.7         | 1.5          | 0.2         | Iris-setosa      |
| 5.0          | 3.3         | 1.4          | 0.2         | Iris-setosa      |
| 7.0          | 3.2         | 4.7          | 1.4         | Iris-versicolor  |
| 6.4          | 3.2         | 4.5          | 1.5         | Iris-versicolor  |
| 6.9          | 3.1         | 4.9          | 1.5         | Iris-versicolor  |
|--------------+-------------+--------------+-------------+------------------|
```

Note that we're merely using sed to only print the header and the first three body rows that belonged to the second file in order to illustrate success. While this method works, it's easier (and less prone to errors) to use csvstack (Groskopf, 2014):

```
$ csvstack Iris-*.csv | sed -n '1p;49,54p' | csvlook
|--------------+-------------+--------------+-------------+------------------|
| sepal_length | sepal_width | petal_length | petal_width | species          |
|--------------+-------------+--------------+-------------+------------------|
| 4.6          | 3.2         | 1.4          | 0.2         | Iris-setosa      |
| 5.3          | 3.7         | 1.5          | 0.2         | Iris-setosa      |
| 5.0          | 3.3         | 1.4          | 0.2         | Iris-setosa      |
| 7.0          | 3.2         | 4.7          | 1.4         | Iris-versicolor  |
| 6.4          | 3.2         | 4.5          | 1.5         | Iris-versicolor  |
| 6.9          | 3.1         | 4.9          | 1.5         | Iris-versicolor  |
|--------------+-------------+--------------+-------------+------------------|
```

If the species column did not exist, you could have created a new column based on the filename using csvstack:

```
$ csvstack Iris-*.csv -n species --filenames
```

Alternatively, you could specify the group names using -g:

```
$ csvstack Iris-*.csv -n class -g a,b,c | csvcut -C species |
> sed -n '1p;49,54p' | csvlook
|-------+--------------+-------------+--------------+-------------|
| class | sepal_length | sepal_width | petal_length | petal_width |
|-------+--------------+-------------+--------------+-------------|
| a     | 4.6          | 3.2         | 1.4          | 0.2         |
| a     | 5.3          | 3.7         | 1.5          | 0.2         |
| a     | 5.0          | 3.3         | 1.4          | 0.2         |
| b     | 7.0          | 3.2         | 4.7          | 1.4         |
| b     | 6.4          | 3.2         | 4.5          | 1.5         |
| b     | 6.9          | 3.1         | 4.9          | 1.5         |
|-------+--------------+-------------+--------------+-------------|
```

The new column class is added at the front. If you'd like to change the order you can use csvcut as discussed earlier in this section.

Concatenate horizontally

Let's say you have three CSV files that you want to put side by side. We use `tee` (Parker, Stallman, & MacKenzie, 2012) to save the result of `csvcut` in the middle of the pipeline:

```
$ < tips.csv csvcut -c bill,tip | tee bills.csv | head -n 3 | csvlook
|--------+-------|
| bill   | tip   |
|--------+-------|
|  16.99 | 1.01  |
|  10.34 | 1.66  |
|--------+-------|
$ < tips.csv csvcut -c day,time | tee datetime.csv |
> head -n 3 | csvlook
|------+---------|
| day  | time    |
|------+---------|
| Sun  | Dinner  |
| Sun  | Dinner  |
|------+---------|
$ < tips.csv csvcut -c sex,smoker,size | tee customers.csv |
> head -n 3 | csvlook
|---------+--------+-------|
| sex     | smoker | size  |
|---------+--------+-------|
| Female  | No     | 2     |
| Male    | No     | 3     |
|---------+--------+-------|
```

Assuming that the rows line up, you can simply `paste` (Ihnat & MacKenzie, 2012) the files together:

```
$ paste -d, {bills,customers,datetime}.csv | head -n 3 | csvlook
|--------+------+--------+--------+------+-----+---------|
| bill   | tip  | sex    | smoker | size | day | time    |
|--------+------+--------+--------+------+-----+---------|
|  16.99 | 1.01 | Female | No     | 2    | Sun | Dinner  |
|  10.34 | 1.66 | Male   | No     | 3    | Sun | Dinner  |
|--------+------+--------+--------+------+-----+---------|
```

The `-d` option instructs `paste` to use a comma as the delimiter.

Joining

Sometimes data cannot simply be combined by vertical or horizontal concatenation. In some cases, especially in relational databases, the data is spread over multiple tables (or files) in order to minimize redundancy. Imagine we wanted to extend the Iris data set with more information about the three types of Iris flowers, namely the USDA identifier. It so happens that we have a separate CSV file with these identifiers:

```
$ csvlook irismeta.csv
|-------------------+------------------------------------------------+---------|
| species           | wikipedia_url                                  | usda_id |
|-------------------+------------------------------------------------+---------|
| Iris-versicolor   | http://en.wikipedia.org/wiki/Iris_versicolor   | IRVE2   |
| Iris-virginica    | http://en.wikipedia.org/wiki/Iris_virginica    | IRVI    |
| Iris-setosa       |                                                | IRSE    |
|-------------------+------------------------------------------------+---------|
```

What this data set and the Iris data set have in common is the `species` column. We can use `csvjoin` (Groskopf, 2014) to join the two data sets:

```
$ csvjoin -c species iris.csv irismeta.csv | csvcut -c sepal_length,\
> sepal_width,species,usda_id | sed -n '1p;49,54p' | csvlook
|---------------+-------------+-----------------+---------|
| sepal_length  | sepal_width | species         | usda_id |
|---------------+-------------+-----------------+---------|
| 4.6           | 3.2         | Iris-setosa     | IRSE    |
| 5.3           | 3.7         | Iris-setosa     | IRSE    |
| 5.0           | 3.3         | Iris-setosa     | IRSE    |
| 7.0           | 3.2         | Iris-versicolor | IRVE2   |
| 6.4           | 3.2         | Iris-versicolor | IRVE2   |
| 6.9           | 3.1         | Iris-versicolor | IRVE2   |
|---------------+-------------+-----------------+---------|
```

Of course we can also use the SQL approach using `csvsql`, which is, as usual, a bit longer (but potentially much more flexible):

```
$ csvsql --query 'SELECT i.sepal_length, i.sepal_width, i.species, m.usda_id '\
> 'FROM iris i JOIN irismeta m ON (i.species = m.species)' \
> iris.csv irismeta.csv | sed -n '1p;49,54p' | csvlook
|---------------+-------------+-----------------+---------|
| sepal_length  | sepal_width | species         | usda_id |
|---------------+-------------+-----------------+---------|
| 4.6           | 3.2         | Iris-setosa     | IRSE    |
| 5.3           | 3.7         | Iris-setosa     | IRSE    |
| 5.0           | 3.3         | Iris-setosa     | IRSE    |
| 7.0           | 3.2         | Iris-versicolor | IRVE2   |
| 6.4           | 3.2         | Iris-versicolor | IRVE2   |
| 6.9           | 3.1         | Iris-versicolor | IRVE2   |
|---------------+-------------+-----------------+---------|
```

Further Reading

- Molinaro, A. (2005). *SQL Cookbook*. O'Reilly Media.

- Goyvaerts, J., & Levithan, S. (2012). *Regular Expressions Cookbook* (2nd Ed.). O'Reilly Media.

- Dougherty, D., & Robbins, A. (1997) . *sed & awk* (2nd Ed.). O'Reilly Media.

Managing Your Data Workflow

We hope that by now you have come to appreciate that the command line is a very convenient environment for doing data science. You may have noticed that, as a consequence of working at the command line, we:

- Invoke many different commands
- Create custom and ad-hoc command-line tools
- Obtain and generate many (intermediate) files

As this process is of an exploratory nature, our workflow tends to be rather chaotic, which makes it difficult to keep track of what we've done. It's very important that our steps can be reproduced, whether by ourselves or by others. When we, for example, continue with a project from a few weeks earlier, chances are that we have forgotten which commands we have run, on which files, in which order, and with which parameters. Imagine the difficulty of passing on your analysis to a collaborator.

You may recover some lost commands by digging into your Bash history, but this is, of course, not a good approach. A better approach would be to save your commands to a Bash script, such as *run.sh*. This allows you and your collaborators to at least reproduce the analysis. A shell script is, however, a suboptimal approach because:

- It's difficult to read and to maintain.
- Dependencies between steps are unclear.
- Every step gets executed every time, which is inefficient and sometimes undesirable.

This is where Drake comes in handy (Factual, 2014). Drake is command-line tool created by Factual that allows you to:

- Formalize your data workflow steps in terms of input and output dependencies
- Run specific steps of your workflow from the command line
- Use inline code (e.g., Python and R)
- Store and retrieve data from external sources (e.g., S3 and HDFS)

Overview

Managing your data workflow with Drake is the main topic of this chapter. As such, you'll learn about:

- Defining your workflow with a so-called *Drakefile*
- Thinking about your workflow in terms of input and output dependencies
- Building specific targets

Introducing Drake

Drake organizes command execution around data and its dependencies. Your data processing steps are formalized in a separate text file (a workflow). Each step usually has one or more inputs and outputs. Drake automatically resolves their dependencies and determines which commands need to be run and in which order.

This means that when you have, say, an SQL query that takes 10 minutes, it only has to be executed when the result is missing or when the query has changed afterwards. Also, if you want to (re-)run a specific step, Drake only considers (re-)running the steps on which it depends. This can save you a lot of time.

The benefit of having a formalized workflow allows you to easily pick up your project after a few weeks and to collaborate with others. We strongly advise you to do this, even when you think this will be a one-off project, because you'll never know when to run certain steps again, or when you want to reuse certain steps in another project.

Installing Drake

Drake has quite a few dependencies, which makes its installation process rather involved. For the following instructions, we assume that you are on Ubuntu.

 If you're using the Data Science Toolbox, then you already have Drake installed, and you may safely skip this section.

Drake is written in the programming language Clojure, which means that it runs on the Java Virtual Machine (JVM). There are pre-built JARs available, but because Drake is in active development, we'll build it from source. For this, you will need to install Leiningen:

```
$ sudo apt-get install openjdk-6-jdk
$ sudo apt-get install leiningen
```

Then, clone the Drake repository from Factual:

```
$ git clone https://github.com/Factual/drake.git
```

And build the JAR using Leiningen:

```
$ cd drake
$ lein uberjar
```

This creates *drake.jar*. Copy this file to a directory that's on your PATH—for example, *~/.bin*:

```
$ mv drake.jar ~/.bin/
```

At this point, you should already be able to run Drake:

```
$ cd ~/.bin/
$ java -jar drake.jar
```

This is not really convenient for two reasons: (1) the Java Virtual Machine (JVM) takes a long time to start, and (2) you can only run it from that directory. We advise you to install Drip, which is a launcher for the JVM that provides much faster startup times than the `java` command. First, clone the Drip repository from Flatland:

```
$ git clone https://github.com/flatland/drip.git
$ cd drip
$ make prefix=~/.bin install
```

Then, create a Bash script that allows you to run Drake from everywhere:

```
$ cd ~/.bin
$ cat << 'EOF' > drake
> #!/bin/bash
> drip -cp $(dirname $0)/drake.jar drake.core "$@"
> EOF
$ chmod +x drake
```

To verify that you have correctly installed both Drake and Drip, you can run the following command, preferably from a different directory:

```
$ drake --version
Drake Version 0.1.6
```

Drip speeds up Java because it reserves an instance of the JVM after it has been run once. Because of this, you will only notice the speed up from the second time onwards.

Obtain Top Ebooks from Project Gutenberg

For the remainder of this chapter, we'll use the following task as a running example. Our goal is to turn the command that we use to solve this task into a Drake workflow. We start out simple, and work our way towards an advanced workflow in order to explain to you the various concepts and syntax of Drake.

Project Gutenberg is an ambitious project that, since 1971, has archived and digitized over 42,000 books that are available online for free. On its website you can find the top 100 most downloaded ebooks. Let's assume that we're interested in the top 5 downloads of Project Gutenberg. Because this list is available in HTML (and formatted in such a way that we don't need scrape), it's straightforward to obtain the top 5 downloads:

```
$ cd ~/book/ch06
$ curl -s 'http://www.gutenberg.org/browse/scores/top' |     ❶
> grep -E '^<li>' |                                          ❷
> head -n 5 |                                                ❸
> sed -E "s/.*ebooks\/([0-9]+).*/\\1/" > data/top-5          ❹
```

This command:

❶   Downloads the HTML.

❷   Extracts the list items.

❸   Keeps only the top 5 items.

❹   Saves ebook IDs to *data/top-5*.

The output of the command is:

```
$ cat data/top-5
1342
76
11
1661
1952
```

If you want to be able to reproduce this at a later time, the easiest thing you can do is put this command in a script as we saw in Chapter 4. If you execute this script again, the HTML will be downloaded again as well. There are three common reasons why you might want to be able to control whether certain steps are run. First, because a step may take a very long time. Second, because you want to continue with the same data. Third, the data may come from an API that has certain rate limits. It would be a good idea to let one step save the data to a file and then let subsequent steps operate on that file so that you don't have to make any redundant computations or API calls. Now, the first reason isn't really a problem in our example because the HTML can be downloaded fast enough. However, in some cases, the data may come from other sources or may comprise gigabytes of data.

Every Workflow Starts with a Single Step

In this section, we'll convert the preceding command to a Drake workflow. A workflow is just a text file. You'd usually name this file *Drakefile* because Drake uses that file if no other file is specified at the command line. A workflow with just a single step would look like Example 6-1.

Example 6-1. A workflow with just a single step (Drakefile)

```
data/top-5 <-                                                    ❶
    curl -s 'http://www.gutenberg.org/browse/scores/top' |       ❷
    grep -E '^<li>' |                                            ❸
    head -n 5 |                                                  ❹
    sed -E "s/.*ebooks\/([0-9]+).*/\\1/" > data/top-5            ❺
```

Let's go through this file. The first line, which contains the arrow pointing to the left, is our step definition. The left side of this arrow, which says *top-5*, is the name or output of this step. Any inputs to this step would appear on the right side of this arrow, but because this step has no input, it's empty. Defining inputs and outputs is what allows Drake to recognize the dependencies between steps, and to figure out whether and when which steps need to be executed in order to fulfill a certain output. This output is also known as a *target*. As you can see, the body of this step is literally our command from before but then indented.

❶ The arrow (<-) denotes the name of the step and its dependencies. More on this later.

❷ The body is indented.

❸ Select only list items.

❹ Get the first 5 items.

❺ Extract the ID, and save to file *top-5*. Note that *top-5* was already specified in the step definition and that 5 has now been used three times. We're going to address that later.

This workflow is as simple as it gets. It doesn't offer any advantages over having our command in a Bash script. But don't worry, we promise you that it will get more exciting. For now, let's run Drake and see what it does with our first workflow:

```
$ drake
The following steps will be run, in order:
  1: data/top-5 <-  [missing output]
Confirm? [y/n] y
Running 1 steps with concurrence of 1...

--- 0. Running (missing output): data/top-5 <-
--- 0: data/top-5 <-  -> done in 0.35s
Done (1 steps run).
```

Between steps, you may want to remove the file *drake.log*, the hidden directory *.drake* and any output files to force Drake to start over.

If we do not specify a workflow file, then Drake will use *./Drakefile*. Drake first determines which steps need to be run. In our case, the one and only step will be run because it's missing the output. This means that there's no file named *data/top-5*. Drake asks for confirmation before it will execute these steps. We press **<Enter>**, and very soon thereafter we see that Drake is done. Drake did not complain about any errors in our steps. Let's verify that we have the top 5 books by looking at the output file *data/top-5*:

```
$ cat data/top-5
1342
76
11
1661
1952
```

Now we do have the output file. Let's run Drake again:

```
$ drake
The following steps will be run, in order:
  1: data/top-5 <-  [no-input step]
Confirm? [y/n] n
Aborted.
```

As you can see, Drake wants to execute the step again! However, it now mentions a different reason, namely, that there's no input step (`[no-input-step]`). Its default behavior is to check whether the input has changed by looking at the timestamp of the input. However, because we didn't specify any input, Drake doesn't know whether or not this step should be run again. We can disable this default behavior to check timestamps as in Example 6-2.

Example 6-2. Drake workflow with timecheck (01.drake)

```
data/top-5 <- [-timecheck]
    curl -s 'http://www.gutenberg.org/browse/scores/top' |
    grep -E '^<li>' |
    head -n 5 |
    sed -E "s/.*ebooks\/([0-9]+)\">([^<]+)<.*/\\1,\\2/" > data/top-5
```

The square brackets indicate that this is an option to the step. The minus (-) in front of timecheck means that we wish to disable checking timestamps. Now, this step is only run when the output is missing.

Let's use different filenames so that we keep old versions. We can specify a different workflow name (other than *Drakefile*) with the -w option. Let's run Drake once more:

```
$ mv Drakefile 01.drake
$ drake -w 01.drake
Nothing to do.
```

Our very first workflow is already saving us time because Drake detects that the step was not need to be executed again. However, we can do much better than this. This workflow has three shortcomings that we're going to address in the next section.

Well, That Depends

Our workflow contains just a single step, which means that, just like having a simple Bash script, everything will be executed all the time. So the first thing we are going to do is to split up this single step into two steps, where the first step downloads the HTML, and the second step processes this HTML. The second step obviously depends on the first step. We can define this dependency in our workflow.

You may have noticed that the number 5 is specified three times. If you ever wanted to get the top, say, top 10 ebooks from Project Gutenberg, we would have to change our workflow in three places. This is inefficient and needs to be addressed. Luckily, Drake supports variables.

It may not be immediately obvious from our workflow, but our data resides in the same location as the script. It's better to have the data live in a separate location and have it separated from any code that generates this data. Not only does it keep our project cleaner, it also allows us to delete the generated data files easier, and we can easily specify that we do not like the data files to be included in any version control system such as git (Torvalds & Hamano, 2014). Let's have a look at our improved workflow in Example 6-3.

Example 6-3. Drake workflow with dependencies (02.drake)

```
NUM:=5                                                              ❶
BASE=data/                                                          ❷

top.html <- [-timecheck]
    curl -s 'http://www.gutenberg.org/browse/scores/top' > $OUTPUT  ❸

top-$[NUM] <- top.html                                             ❹
    < $INPUT grep -E '^<li>' |
    head -n $[NUM] |
    sed -E "s/.*ebooks\/([0-9]+)\">([^<]+)<.*/\\1,\\2/" > $OUTPUT
```

❶ You can specify variables in Drake, preferably at the beginning of the file, by specifying the variable name, then an equal sign, and then the value. The name of the variable doesn't have to be in all capitals, but it does make them stand out more. As you can see, we have used for the variable NUM the notation := instead of =. This means that if the variable NUM is already set, it will not be overridden. This allows us to specify the value of NUM from the command line before we run Drake.

❷ The BASE variable is a special variable. Drake will treat every file specified in the workflow as if it were in this base directory.

❸ We now have two steps. The first step has the same input as before, but now the output is a different file, namely, *top.html*. This output is defined again as the input of step 2. This is how Drake knows that the second step depends on the first step.

❹ We have used two more special variables: INPUT and OUTPUT. Values of these two special variables are set to what we have defined as the input and output of that step, respectively. This way we don't have to specify the input and output of a certain step twice. Furthermore, it allows us to easily reuse certain steps in future workflows.

Let's execute this new workflow using Drake:

```
$ drake -w 02.drake
The following steps will be run, in order:
  1: data/top.html <-  [missing output]
  2: data/top-5 <- data/top.html [projected timestamped]
Confirm? [y/n] y
Running 2 steps with concurrence of 1...

--- 0. Running (missing output): data/top.html <-
--- 0: data/top.html <-  -> done in 0.89s

--- 1. Running (missing output): data/top-5 <- data/top.html
```

```
--- 1: data/top-5 <- data/top.html -> done in 0.02s
Done (2 steps run).
```

Now, let's assume that we want instead of the top 5 ebooks, the top 10 ebooks. We can set the NUM variable from the command line and run Drake (Example 6-4).

Example 6-4. Drake workflow with NUM=10 (02.drake)

```
$ NUM=10 drake -w 02.drake
The following steps will be run, in order:
  1: data/top-10 <- data/top.html [missing output]
Confirm? [y/n] y
Running 1 steps with concurrence of 1...

--- 1. Running (missing output): data/top-10 <- data/top.html
--- 1: data/top-10 <- data/top.html -> done in 0.02s
Done (1 steps run).
```

As you can see, Drake now only needs to execute the second step, because the output of the first step has already been satisfied. Again, downloading an HTML file is not such a big deal, but can you imagine the implications if you were dealing with 10 GB worth of data?

Rebuilding Specific Targets

The list of the top 100 ebooks on project Gutenberg changes daily. We've seen that if we run the Drake workflow again, the HTML containing this list is not downloaded again. Luckily, Drake allows us to run certain steps again so that we can update this HTML file:

```
$ drake -w 02.drake '=top.html'
```

There is a more convenient way than using the output filename to specify which step you want to execute again. We can add so-called *tags* to both the input and output of steps. A tag starts with a %. It's a good idea to choose a short and descriptive tag name so that you can easily specify this at the command line. Let's add the tag %html to the first step and %filter to the second step, as in Example 6-5.

Example 6-5. Drake workflow with tags (03.drake)

```
NUM:=5
BASE=data/

top.html, %html <- [-timecheck]
    curl -s 'http://www.gutenberg.org/browse/scores/top' > $OUTPUT

top-$[NUM], %filter <- top.html
    < $INPUT grep -E '^<li>' |
```

```
head -n $[NUM] |
sed -E "s/.*ebooks\/([0-9]+)\">([^<]+)<.*/\\1,\\2/" > $OUTPUT
```

We can now rebuild the first step by specifying the %html tag:

```
$ drake -w 03.drake '=%html'
```

Discussion

One of the beauties of the command line is that it allows you to play with your data. You can easily execute different commands and process different datafiles. It's a very interactive and iterative process. After a while, it is easy to forget which steps you have taken to get the desired result. It's therefore very important to document your steps every once in a while. This way, if you or one of your collaborators picks up your project after some time, the same result can be produced again by executing the same steps.

This chapter has shown that just putting every command in one Bash script is suboptimal. We have proposed to use Drake as a command-line tool to manage your data workflow. By using a running example, we have shown you how to define steps and the dependencies between them. We've also discussed how to use variables and tags.

There's nothing more fun than just playing with your data and forgetting everything else. But trust us when we say that it's worthwhile to keep a record of what you have done (by means of a Drake workflow). Not only will it make your life easier, but you will also start thinking about your data workflow in terms of steps. Just as with your own data science toolbox—which you expand over time, making you more efficient —Drake workflows also make for a more organized setup. The more steps you have defined, the easier it gets to keep doing it, because very often you can reuse certain steps. We hope that you will get used to Drake, and that it'll make your life easier.

This chapter has only scratch the surface of all Drake has to offer. Some of its more advanced features are:

- Asynchronous execution of steps
- Support for inline Python and R code
- Upload and download data from HDFS and S3

Further Reading

- Factual. (2014). Drake. Retrieved from *https://github.com/Factual/drake*.

Exploring Data

Now that we have obtained and scrubbed our data, we can continue with the third step of the OSEMN model, which is to explore it. After all that hard work (unless you already had clean data lying around!), it's time for some fun.

Exploring is the step where you familiarize yourself with the data. Being familiar with the data is essential when you want to extract any value from it. For example, knowing what kind of features the data has, means you know which ones are worth further exploring and which ones you can use to answer any questions that you have.

Exploring your data can be done from three perspectives. The first perspective is to inspect the data and its properties. Here, we want to know, for example, what the raw data looks like, how many data points the data set has, and what kind of features the data set has.

The second perspective from which we can explore out data is to compute descriptive statistics. This perspective is useful for learning more about the individual features. One advantage of this perspective is that the output is often brief and textual and can therefore be printed on the command line.

The third perspective is to create visualizations of the data. From this perspective, we can gain insight into how multiple features interact. We'll discuss a way of creating visualizations that can be printed on the command line. However, most visualizations are best displayed on graphical user interfaces. An advantage of visualizations over descriptive statistics is that visualizations are more flexible and can convey much more information.

Overview

In this chapter, you'll learn how to:

- Inspect the data and its properties
- Compute descriptive statistics
- Create data visualizations inside and outside the command line

Inspecting Data and Its Properties

In this section, we'll demonstrate how to inspect a data set and its properties. Because the upcoming visualization and modeling techniques expect the data to be in tabular form, we'll assume that the data is in CSV format. You can use the techniques described in Chapter 5 to convert your data to CSV if necessary.

For simplicity's sake, we'll also assume that your data has a header. In the first subsection, we are going to determine whether that is the case. Once we know we have the data in place, we can continue answering the following questions:

- How many data points and features does the data set have?
- What does the raw data look like?
- What kind of features does the data set have?
- Can some of these features be treated as categorical or as factors?

Header or Not, Here I Come

You can check whether your file has a header by printing the first few lines:

```
$ head file.csv | csvlook
```

It's then up to you to decide whether the first line is indeed a header or already the first data point. When the data set contains no header or when its header contains newlines, you're best off going back and correcting that by scrubbing the date (refer to Chapter 5 for information on how to do that).

Inspect All the Data

If you want to inspect the raw data, then it's best not to use the `cat` command-line tool, as `cat` prints all the data to the screen in one go. In order to inspect the raw data at your own pace, we recommend using `less` (Nudelman, 2013) with the `-S` option:

```
$ less -S file.csv
```

The -S option ensures that long lines are not being wrapped when they don't fit in the terminal. Instead, less allows you to scroll horizontally to see the rest of the lines. The advantage of less is that it does not load the entire file into memory, which is good for viewing large files. Once you're in less, you can scroll down a full screen by pressing **<Space>**. Scrolling horizontally is done by pressing **<Left>** and **<Right>**. Press **g** and **G** to go to start and the end of the file, respectively. Quitting less is done by pressing **q**. Read the man page for more key bindings.

If you want the data set to be nicely formatted, you can add csvlook to the pipeline:

```
$ < file.csv csvlook | less -S
```

 Unfortunately, csvlook needs to read the entire file into memory in order to determine the width of the columns. So, when you want to inspect a very large file, you may want to get a subset (using sample, for instance) or you may need to be patient.

Feature Names and Data Types

In order to gain insight into the data set, it is useful to print the feature names and study them. After all, the feature names may indicate the meaning of the feature. You can use the following sed expression for this:

```
$ cd ~/book/ch07
$ < data/iris.csv sed -e 's/,/\n/g;q'
sepal_length
sepal_width
petal_length
petal_width
species
```

Note that this basic command assumes that the file is delimited by commas. Just as a reminder, if you intend to use this command often, you could define a function in your ~/.bashrc file called, say, names:

```
names () { sed -e 's/,/\n/g;q'; }
```

Which you can then use like this:

```
$ < data/investments2.csv names
company_permalink
company_name
company_category_list
company_market
company_country_code
company_state_code
company_region
company_city
investor_permalink
```

```
investor_name
investor_category_list
investor_market
investor_country_code
investor_state_code
investor_region
investor_city
funding_round_permalink
funding_round_type
funding_round_code
funded_at
funded_month
funded_quarter
funded_year
raised_amount_usd
```

We can go a step further than just printing the column names. Besides the names of the columns, it would be very useful to know what type of values each column contains. Examples of data types are a string of characters, a numerical value, or a date. Assume that we have the following toy data set:

```
$ < data/datatypes.csv csvlook
|-----+--------+-------+----------+------------------+------------+----------|
| a   | b      | c     | d        | e                | f          | g        |
|-----+--------+-------+----------+------------------+------------+----------|
| 2   | 0.0    | FALSE | "Yes!"   | 2011-11-11 11:00 | 2012-09-08 | 12:34    |
| 42  | 3.1415 | TRUE  | Oh, good | 2014-09-15       | 12/6/70    | 0:07 PM  |
| 66  |        | False | 2198     |                  |            |          |
|-----+--------+-------+----------+------------------+------------+----------|
```

We've already used csvsql in Chapter 5 to execute SQL queries directly on CSV data. When no command-line arguments are passed, it generates the SQL statement that would be needed if we were to insert this data into an actual database. We can use the output also for ourselves to inspect what the inferred column types are:

```
csvsql data/datatypes.csv
CREATE TABLE datatypes (
        a INTEGER NOT NULL,
        b FLOAT,
        c BOOLEAN NOT NULL,
        d VARCHAR(8) NOT NULL,
        e DATETIME,
        f DATE,
        g TIME,
        CHECK (c IN (0, 1))
);
```

Table 7-1 provides an overview of what the various SQL data types mean. If a column has the *NOT NULL* string printed after the data type, that column contains no missing values in the data set.

Table 7-1. Python versus SQL data types

Type	Python	SQL
Character string	unicode	VARCHAR
Boolean	bool	BOOLEAN
Integer	int	INTEGER
Real number	float	FLOAT
Date	datetime.date	DATE
Time	datetime.time	TIME
Date and time	datetime.datetime	DATETIME

Unique Identifiers, Continuous Variables, and Factors

Knowing the data type of each feature is not enough. It's also essential to know what each feature represents. Having knowledge about the domain is very useful here, however we may also get some ideas from the data itself.

Both a string and an integer could be a unique identifier or could represent a category. In the latter case, this could be used to assign a color to your visualization. If an integer denotes, say, the ZIP code, then it doesn't make sense to compute the average.

To determine whether a feature should be treated as a unique identifier or categorical variable (or *factor* in R terminology), you could count the number of unique values for a specific column:

```
$ cat data/iris.csv | csvcut -c species | body "sort | uniq | wc -l"
species
3
```

Or we can use `csvstat` (Groskopf, 2014), which is part of Csvkit, to get the number of unique values for each column:

```
$ csvstat data/investments2.csv --unique
 1. company_permalink: 27342
 2. company_name: 27324
 3. company_category_list: 8759
 4. company_market: 443
 5. company_country_code: 150
 6. company_state_code: 147
 7. company_region: 1079
 8. company_city: 3305
 9. investor_permalink: 11176
10. investor_name: 11135
```

```
11. investor_category_list: 468
12. investor_market: 134
13. investor_country_code: 111
14. investor_state_code: 80
15. investor_region: 549
16. investor_city: 1198
17. funding_round_permalink: 41790
18. funding_round_type: 13
19. funding_round_code: 15
20. funded_at: 3595
21. funded_month: 295
22. funded_quarter: 121
23. funded_year: 34
24. raised_amount_usd: 6143
```

If the number of unique values is low compared to the number of rows in the data set, then that feature may indeed be treated as a categorical one (such as `fund ing_round_type`). If the number is equal to the number of rows, it may be a unique identifier (such as `company_permalink`).

Computing Descriptive Statistics

Using csvstat

The command-line tool `csvstat` gives a lot of information. For each feature it shows:

- The data type in Python terminology (see Table 7-1 for a comparison between Python and SQL data types)
- Whether it has any missing values (`Nulls`)
- The number of unique values
- Various descriptive statistics (i.e., maximum, minimum, sum, mean, standard deviation, and median) for those features for which it's appropriate

We invoke `csvstat` as follows:

```
$ csvstat data/datatypes.csv
  1. a
      <type 'int'>
      Nulls: False
      Values: 2, 66, 42
  2. b
      <type 'float'>
      Nulls: True
      Values: 0.0, 3.1415
  3. c
      <type 'bool'>
      Nulls: False
      Unique values: 2
```

```
          5 most frequent values:
                  False:  2
                  True:   1
  4. d
          <type 'unicode'>
          Nulls: False
          Values: 2198, "Yes!", Oh, good
  5. e
          <type 'datetime.datetime'>
          Nulls: True
          Values: 2011-11-11 11:00:00, 2014-09-15 00:00:00
  6. f
          <type 'datetime.date'>
          Nulls: True
          Values: 2012-09-08, 1970-12-06
  7. g
          <type 'datetime.time'>
          Nulls: True
          Values: 12:34:00, 12:07:00

  Row count: 3
```

This gives a very verbose output. For a more concise output specify one of the statistics options:

- --max (maximum)

- --min (minimum)

- --sum (sum)

- --mean (mean)

- --median (median)

- --stdev (standard deviation)

- --nulls (whether column contains nulls)

- --unique (unique values)

- --freq (frequent values)

- --len (max value length)

For example:

```
$ csvstat data/datatypes.csv --null
  1. a: False
  2. b: True
  3. c: False
  4. d: False
  5. e: True
  6. f: True
  7. g: True
```

You can select a subset of features with the `-c` option. This accepts both integers and column names:

```
$ csvstat data/investments2.csv -c 2,13,19,24
  2. company_name
        <type 'unicode'>
        Nulls: True
        Unique values: 27324
        5 most frequent values:
                Aviir:  13
                Galectin Therapeutics:  12
                Rostima:              12
                Facebook:             11
                Lending Club:    11
        Max length: 66
 13. investor_country_code
        <type 'unicode'>
        Nulls: True
        Unique values: 111
        5 most frequent values:
                USA:      20806
                GBR:      2357
                DEU:      946
                CAN:      893
                FRA:      737
        Max length: 15
 19. funding_round_code
        <type 'unicode'>
        Nulls: True
        Unique values: 15
        5 most frequent values:
                a:        7529
                b:        4776
                c:        2452
                d:        1042
                e:        384
        Max length: 10
 24. raised_amount_usd
        <type 'int'>
        Nulls: True
        Min: 0
        Max: 3200000000
        Sum: 359891203117
        Mean: 10370010.1748
        Median: 3250000
        Standard Deviation: 38513119.1802
        Unique values: 6143
        5 most frequent values:
                10000000:      1159
                1000000:       1074
                5000000:       1066
                2000000:       875
```

```
3000000:          820
```

```
Row count: 41799
```

Note that `csvstat`, just like `csvsql`, employs heuristics to determine the data type, and therefore may not always get it right. We encourage you to always do a manual inspection as discussed in the previous subsection. Moreover, the type may be a character string or integer, but that doesn't say anything about how it should be treated.

As a nice extra, `csvstat` outputs, at the very end, the number of data points. Newlines and commas inside values are handled correctly. To only see the relevant line of the output, we can use `tail`:

```
$ csvstat data/iris.csv | tail -n 1
Row count: 150
```

If you only want to see the actual number of data points, you can use, for example, the following `sed` expression to extract the number:

```
$ csvstat data/iris.csv | sed -rne '${s/^([^:]+): ([0-9]+)$/\2/;p}'
150
```

Using R from the Command Line with Rio

In this section, we'd like to introduce you to a command-line tool called `Rio`, which is essentially a small, nifty wrapper around the statistical programming environment R. Before we explain what `Rio` does and why it exists, lets talk a bit about R itself.

R is a very powerful statistical software package to analyze data and create visualizations. It's an interpreted programming language, has an extensive collection of packages, and offers its own REPL, which allows you, similar to the command line, to play with your data. Unfortunately, R is quite separated from the command line. Once you start it, you're in a separate environment. R doesn't really play well with the command line because you cannot pipe any data into it and it also doesn't support any oneliners that you can specify.

For example, imagine that you have a CSV file called *data/tips.csv*, and you would like to compute the tip percentage and save the result. To accomplish this in R, you would first start up R:

```
$ R
```

And then run the following commands:

```
> tips <- read.csv('data/tips.csv', header = T, sep = ',', stringsAsFactors = F)
> tips.percent <- tips$tip / tips$bill * 100
> cat(tips.percent, sep = '\n', file = 'data/percent.csv')
> q("no")
```

Afterwards, you can continue with the saved file *data/percent.csv* on the command line. Note that there is only one command that is associated with what we want to accomplish specifically. The other commands are necessary boilerplate. Typing in this boilerplate in order to accomplish something simple is cumbersome and breaks your workflow. Sometimes, you only want to do one or two things at a time to your data. Wouldn't it be great if we could harness the power of R and be able to use it from the command line?

This is where `Rio` comes in. The name `Rio` stands for *R input/output*, because it enables you to use R as a filter on the command line. You simply pipe CSV data into `Rio` and you specify the R commands that you want to run on it. Let's perform the same task as before, but now using `Rio`:

```
$ < data/tips.csv Rio -e 'df$tip / df$bill * 100' | head
5.944673
16.05416
16.65873
13.97804
14.68076
18.62396
22.80502
11.60714
13.03191
21.85386
```

`Rio` can execute multiple R commands that are separated by semicolons. So, if you wanted to add a column called *percent* to the input data, you could do the following:

```
$ < data/tips.csv Rio -e 'df$percent <- df$tip / df$bill * 100; df' | head
bill,tip,sex,smoker,day,time,size,percent
16.99,1.01,Female,No,Sun,Dinner,2,5.94467333725721
10.34,1.66,Male,No,Sun,Dinner,3,16.0541586073501
21.01,3.5,Male,No,Sun,Dinner,3,16.6587339362208
23.68,3.31,Male,No,Sun,Dinner,2,13.9780405405405
24.59,3.61,Female,No,Sun,Dinner,4,14.6807645384303
25.29,4.71,Male,No,Sun,Dinner,4,18.6239620403321
8.77,2,Male,No,Sun,Dinner,2,22.8050171037628
26.88,3.12,Male,No,Sun,Dinner,4,11.6071428571429
15.04,1.96,Male,No,Sun,Dinner,2,13.031914893617
```

These small one-liners are possible because `Rio` takes care of all the boilerplate. Being able to use the command line for this and capture the power of R into a one-liner is fantastic, especially if you want to keep on working on the command line. `Rio` assumes that the input data is in CSV format with a header. (By specifying the `-n` option, `Rio` does not consider the first row to be the header and creates default column names.) Behind the scenes, `Rio` writes the piped data to a temporary CSV file and creates a script that:

- Imports required packages
- Loads the CSV file as a `data.frame`
- Generates a `ggplot2` object if needed (more on this in the next section)
- Runs the specified commands
- Prints the result of the last command to standard output

So now, if you wanted to do one or two things to your data set with R, you can specify it as a one-liner, and keep on working on the command line. All the knowledge that you already have about R can now be leveraged from the command line. With `Rio`, you can even create sophisticated visualizations, as you'll see later in this chapter.

Rio doesn't have to be used as a filter, meaning the output doesn't have to be in CSV format per se. You can compute various descriptive statistics:

```
$ < data/iris.csv Rio -e 'mean(df$sepal_length)'
5.843333
$ < data/iris.csv Rio -e 'sd(df$sepal_length)'
0.8280661
$ < data/iris.csv Rio -e 'sum(df$sepal_length)'
876.5
```

And if we wanted to compute the five summary statistics, we would do:

```
$ < data/iris.csv Rio -e 'summary(df$sepal_length)'
   Min. 1st Qu.  Median    Mean 3rd Qu.    Max.
  4.300   5.100   5.800   5.843   6.400   7.900
```

You can also compute the skewness (symmetry of the distribution) and kurtosis (peakedness of the distribution), but then you need to have the `moments` package installed:

```
$ < data/iris.csv Rio -e 'skewness(df$sepal_length)'
$ < data/iris.csv Rio -e 'kurtosis(df$petal_width)'
```

Correlation between two features:

```
$ < dat/iris.csv Rio -e 'cor(df$bill, df$tip)'
0.6757341
```

Or even a correlation matrix:

```
$ < data/tips.csv csvcut -c bill,tip | Rio -f cor | csvlook
|--------------------+--------------------|
|  bill              |  tip               |
|--------------------+--------------------|
|  1                 |  0.675734109211365 |
|  0.675734109211365 |  1                 |
|--------------------+--------------------|
```

Note that with the -f option, we can specify the function to apply to the data.frame df. In this case, it is the same as -e cor(df).

You can even create a stem plot (Tukey, 1977) using Rio:

```
$ < data/iris.csv Rio -e 'stem(df$sepal_length)'

  The decimal point is 1 digit(s) to the left of the |

  42 | 0
  44 | 0000
  46 | 000000
  48 | 0000000000
  50 | 000000000000000000000
  52 | 00000
  54 | 0000000000000
  56 | 00000000000000
  58 | 0000000000
  60 | 000000000000
  62 | 0000000000000
  64 | 000000000000
  66 | 0000000000
  68 | 0000000
  70 | 00
  72 | 0000
  74 | 0
  76 | 00000
  78 | 0
```

Creating Visualizations

In this section, we're going to discuss how to create visualizations at the command line. We'll be looking at two different software packages: Gnuplot and ggplot2. First, we'll introduce both packages, and then we'll demonstrate how to create several different types of visualizations using both of them.

Introducing Gnuplot and feedgnuplot

The first software package to create visualizations that we're discussing in this chapter is Gnuplot, which has been around since 1986. Despite being rather old, its visualization capabilities are quite extensive. As such, it's impossible to do it justice in one section. There are already good resources available, including *Gnuplot in Action* by Janert (2009).

To demonstrate the flexibility (and its archaic notation), consider Example 7-1, which is copied from the Gnuplot website (*http://gnuplot.sourceforge.net/demo/histograms. 6.gnu*).

Example 7-1. Creating a histogram using Gnuplot

```
# set terminal pngcairo  transparent enhanced font "arial,10" fontscale 1.0 size
# set output 'histograms.6.png'
set border 3 front linetype -1 linewidth 1.000
set boxwidth 0.75 absolute
set style fill   solid 1.00 border lt -1
set grid nopolar
set grid noxtics nomxtics ytics nomytics noztics nomztics \
 nox2tics nomx2tics noy2tics nomy2tics nocbtics nomcbtics
set grid layerdefault   linetype 0 linewidth 1.000,  linetype 0 linewidth 1.000
set key outside right top vertical Left reverse noenhanced autotitles columnhead
set style histogram columnstacked title  offset character 0, 0, 0
set datafile missing '-'
set style data histograms
set xtics border in scale 1,0.5 nomirror norotate  offset character 0, 0, 0 auto
set xtics   norangelimit
set xtics    ()
set ytics border in scale 0,0 mirror norotate  offset character 0, 0, 0 autojust
set ztics border in scale 0,0 nomirror norotate  offset character 0, 0, 0 autoju
set cbtics border in scale 0,0 mirror norotate  offset character 0, 0, 0 autojus
set rtics axis in scale 0,0 nomirror norotate  offset character 0, 0, 0 autojust
set title "Immigration from Northern Europe\n(columstacked histogram)"
set xlabel "Country of Origin"
set ylabel "Immigration by decade"
set yrange [ 0.00000 : * ] noreverse nowriteback
i = 23
plot 'immigration.dat' using 6 ti col, '' using 12 ti col,      '' using 13 ti c
```

Note that this is trimmed to 80 characters wide. This script generates the plot shown in Figure 7-1.

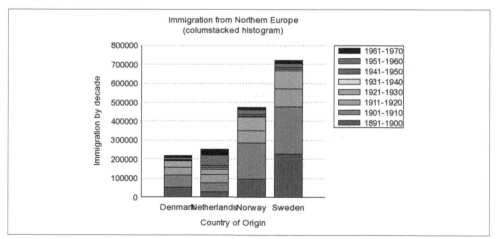

Figure 7-1. Immigration plot by Gnuplot

Gnuplot is different from most command-line tools we've been using for two reasons. First, it uses a script instead of command-line arguments. Second, the output is always written to a file and not printed to standard output.

One great advantage of Gnuplot being around for so long, and the main reason we've included it in this book, is that it's able to produce visualizations *for* the command line. That is, it's able to print its output to the terminal without the need for a GUI. Even then, you would still need to set up a script.

Luckily, there is a command-line tool called `feedgnuplot` (Kogan, 2014), which can help us with setting up a script for Gnuplot. `feedgnuplot` is entirely configurable through command-line arguments. Plus, it reads from standard input. After we have introduced `ggplot2`, we're going to create a few visualizations using `feedgnuplot`.

One great feature of `feedgnuplot` that we would like to mention here, is that it allows you to plot streaming data. The following is a snapshot of a continuously updated plot based on random input data:

```
$ while true; do echo $RANDOM; done | sample -d 10 | feedgnuplot --stream \
> --terminal 'dumb 80,25' --lines --xlen 10
```

```
30000 ++-----+------------+------------+------------+------------+-----++
      |       +            *            +            +            +      |
      |       :           **            :           *******       :      *
25000 ++...............*.*...........................*......*...........+*
      |       :         *: *            :           *:      *      :     *|
      |       :         *: *            :           *:      *      :     *|
      |       :        * :  *           :          * :      *      :    * |
20000 ++..............*.....*...........................*..........*......*++
      |       :       * :    *          :         *  :      *      :    * |
      |       :      * :    *           :         *  :     *       :   *  |
15000 ++....**.........*.......*..................*.........*.......*.++
      | **** :*        *  :     *        :         *  :      *   :    * |
      **     :*        *  :      *       ****      *   :      *   :  *  |
10000 ++........*......*....*.......*..**....*....*.........*.....*..++
      |       : *       *   :      * **  :  *   *    :          *  : *    |
      |       : *       *   :      **    :  ** *     :          *  : *    |
      |       : *     *     :            :     *     :          *  : *    |
 5000 ++..........*..*...................................*.....*.*....++
      |       :     * *    :            :           :           *:*      |
      |       +     **      +           +           +           *        |
    0 ++-----+------*-----+------------+------------+------------*-----++
            2350         2352         2354         2356         2358
```

Introducing ggplot2

A more modern software package for creating visualizations is `ggplot2`, which is an implementation of the grammar of graphics in R (Wickham, 2009).

Thanks to the grammar of graphics and using sensible defaults, ggplot2 commands tend to be very short and expressive. When used through Rio, this is a very convenient way of creating visualizations from the command line.

To demonstrate its expressiveness, we'll re-create the histogram plot we earlier generated using Gnuplot, with the help of Rio. Because Rio expects the data set to be comma-delimited, and because ggplot2 expects the data in *long* format, we first need to scrub and transform the data a little bit:

```
$ < data/immigration.dat sed -re '/^#/d;s/\t/,/g;s/,-,/,0,/g;s/Region/'\
> 'Period/' | tee data/immigration.csv | head | cut -c1-80
Period,Austria,Hungary,Belgium,Czechoslovakia,Denmark,France,Germany,Greece,Irel
1891-1900,234081,181288,18167,0,50231,30770,505152,15979,388416,651893,26758,950
1901-1910,668209,808511,41635,0,65285,73379,341498,167519,339065,2045877,48262,1
1911-1920,453649,442693,33746,3426,41983,61897,143945,184201,146181,1109524,4371
1921-1930,32868,30680,15846,102194,32430,49610,412202,51084,211234,455315,26948,
1931-1940,3563,7861,4817,14393,2559,12623,144058,9119,10973,68028,7150,4740,3960
1941-1950,24860,3469,12189,8347,5393,38809,226578,8973,19789,57661,14860,10100,1
1951-1960,67106,36637,18575,918,10984,51121,477765,47608,43362,185491,52277,2293
1961-1970,20621,5401,9192,3273,9201,45237,190796,85969,32966,214111,30606,15484,
```

The sed expression consists of four parts, delimited by semicolons:

1. Remove lines that start with a comment (#).
2. Convert tabs to commas.
3. Change dashes (missing values) into zero's.
4. Change the feature name Region into Period.

We then select only the columns that matter using csvcut and subsequently convert the data from a wide format to a long one using the Rio and the melt function which is part of the R package reshape2:

```
$ < data/immigration.csv csvcut -c Period,Denmark,Netherlands,Norway,\
> Sweden | Rio -re 'melt(df, id="Period", variable.name="Country", '\
> 'value.name="Count")' | tee data/immigration-long.csv | head | csvlook
|-----------+-------------+-------|
| Period    | Country     | Count |
|-----------+-------------+-------|
| 1891-1900 | Denmark     | 50231 |
| 1901-1910 | Denmark     | 65285 |
| 1911-1920 | Denmark     | 41983 |
| 1921-1930 | Denmark     | 32430 |
| 1931-1940 | Denmark     | 2559  |
| 1941-1950 | Denmark     | 5393  |
| 1951-1960 | Denmark     | 10984 |
| 1961-1970 | Denmark     | 9201  |
| 1891-1900 | Netherlands | 26758 |
|-----------+-------------+-------|
```

Now, we can use `Rio` again, but with an expression that builds up a `ggplot2` visualization:

```
$ < data/immigration-long.csv Rio -ge 'g + geom_bar(aes(Country, Count,'\
> ' fill=Period), stat="identity") + scale_fill_brewer(palette="Set1") '\
> '+ labs(x="Country of origin", y="Immigration by decade", title='\
> '"Immigration from Northern Europe\n(columstacked histogram)")' | display
```

The `-g` option specifies that `Rio` should load the `ggplot2` package. The output is an image in PNG format (Figure 7-2). You can view the PNG image via `display`, which is part of ImageMagick (ImageMagick Studio LLC, 2009) or you can redirect the output to a PNG file. If you're on a remote terminal then you probably won't be able to see any graphics. A workaround for this is to launch a web server from a particular directory:

```
$ python -m SimpleHTTPServer 8000
```

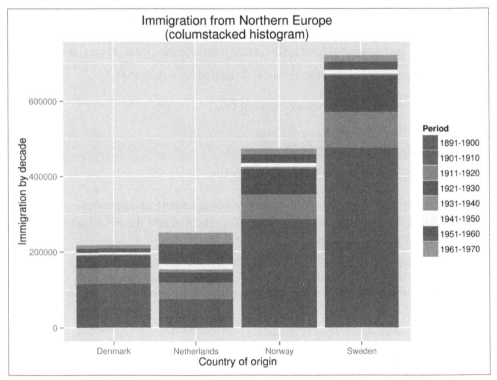

Figure 7-2. Immigration plot by Rio and ggplot2

Make sure that you have access to the port (8000, in this case). If you save the PNG image to the directory from which the web server was launched, then you can access the image from your browser at *http://localhost:8000/file.png*.

Histograms

Using Rio (Figure 7-3):

```
$ < data/tips.csv Rio -ge 'g+geom_histogram(aes(bill))' | display
```

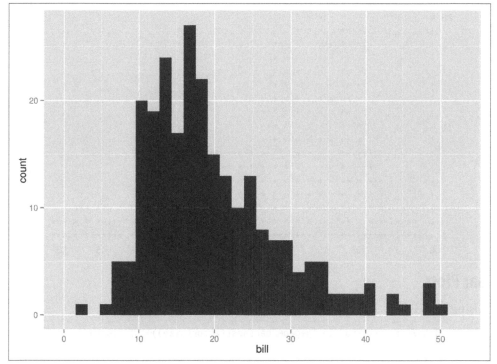

Figure 7-3. Histogram

Using `feedgnuplot`:

```
$ < data/tips.csv csvcut -c bill | feedgnuplot --terminal 'dumb 80,25' \
> --histogram 0 --with boxes --ymin 0 --binwidth 1.5 --unset grid --exit
```

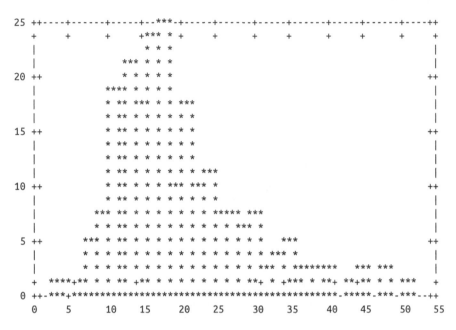

Bar Plots

Using `Rio` (Figure 7-4):

```
$ < data/tips.csv Rio -ge 'g+geom_bar(aes(factor(size)))' | display
```

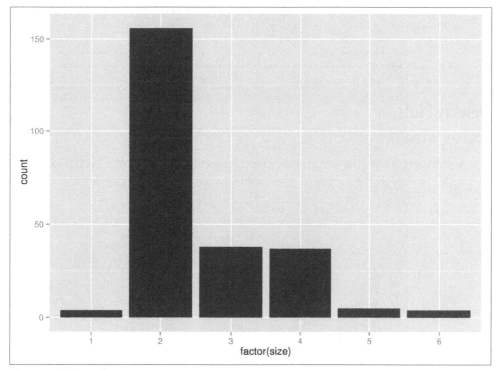

Figure 7-4. Bar plot

Using `feedgnuplot`:

```
$ < data/tips.csv | csvcut -c size | header -d | feedgnuplot --terminal \
> 'dumb 80,25' --histogram 0  --with boxes --unset grid --exit
```

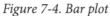

```
160 ++--------+----***********----+---------+---------+---------+--------++
    +        +     *    +    *    +         +         +         +        +
140 ++             *         *                                          ++
    |              *         *                                           |
    |              *         *                                           |
120 ++             *         *                                          ++
    |              *         *                                           |
100 ++             *         *                                          ++
    |              *         *                                           |
    |              *         *                                           |
 80 ++             *         *                                          ++
    |              *         *                                           |
 60 ++             *         *                                          ++
    |              *         *                                           |
    |              *         *                                           |
 40 ++             *         *********************                      ++
```

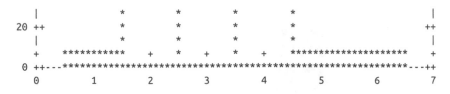

Density Plots

Using `Rio` (Figure 7-5):

```
$ < data/tips.csv Rio -ge 'g+geom_density(aes(tip / bill * 100, fill=sex), '\
> 'alpha=0.3) + xlab("percent")' | display
```

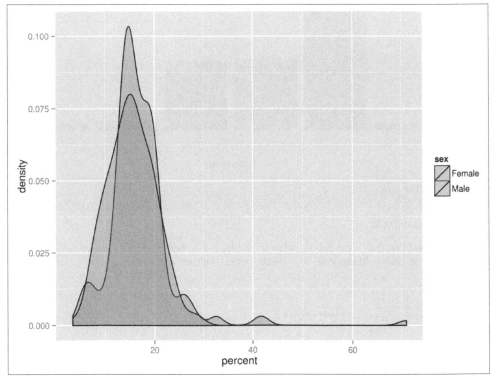

Figure 7-5. Density plot

`feedgnuplot` cannot generate density plots, so it's best to just generate a histogram.

Box Plots

Using Rio:

```
$ < data/tips.csv Rio -ge 'g+geom_boxplot(aes(time, bill))' | display
```

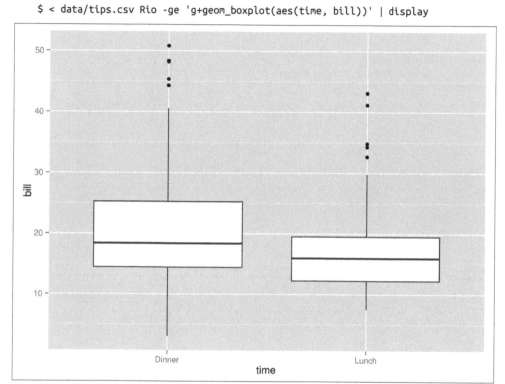

Figure 7-6. Box plot

Drawing a box plot is unfortunately not possible with feedgnuplot.

Scatter Plots

Using Rio (Figure 7-7):

```
$ < data/tips.csv Rio -ge 'g+geom_point(aes(bill, tip, color=time))' | display
```

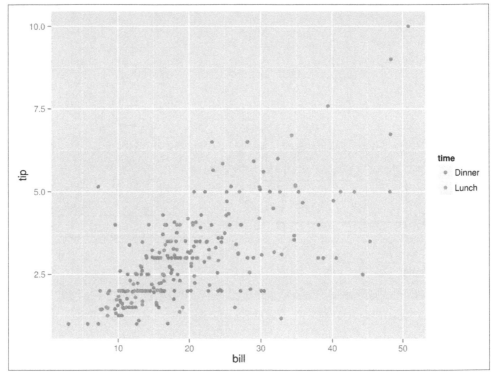

Figure 7-7. Scatter plot

Using `feedgnuplot`:

```
$ < data/tips.csv csvcut -c bill,tip | tr , ' ' | header -d | feedgnuplot \
> --terminal 'dumb 80,25' --points --domain --unset grid --exit --style pt 14
```

```
  10 ++----+------+-----+------+-----+------+-----+------+-----+------+A---++
     +     +      +     +      +     +      +     +      +     +      +     +
   9 ++                                                            A      ++
     |                                                                    |
   8 ++                                                                   ++
     |                                                A                    |
     |                                                                     |
   7 ++                                       A                A         ++
     |                         A     A                                     |
```

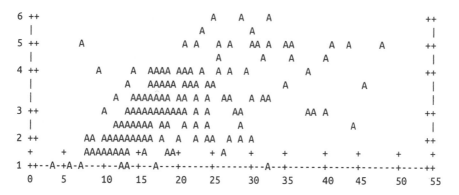

```
6 ++                    A    A    A                        ++
  |                 A         A                            |
5 ++      A              A A  A A    AA A  AA      A  A    A     ++
  |                      A      A    A      A              |
4 ++       A       A  AAAA AAA A  A  A   A         A       ++
  |             A    AAAAA AAA AA          A            A  |
  |          A  AAAAAAA AA A A   AA    A AA                |
3 ++       A    AAAAAAAAAAA A A     AA        AA A         ++
  |             AAAAAAA AA  A A A      A             A     |
2 ++      AA AAAAAAAAA A  A  A AA  A A A                   ++
  +     +   AAAAAAAA +A   AA+    + A   +    +    +    +    +
1 ++--A-+A-A---+--AA-+--A---+-----+-----+--A--+-----+-----+----++
  0    5    10   15   20   25   30   35   40   45   50   55
```

Line Graphs

Using Rio (Figure 7-8):

```
$ < data/immigration-long.csv Rio -ge 'g+geom_line(aes(x=Period, '\
> 'y=Count, group=Country, color=Country)) + theme(axis.text.x = '\
> 'element_text(angle = -45, hjust = 0))' | display
```

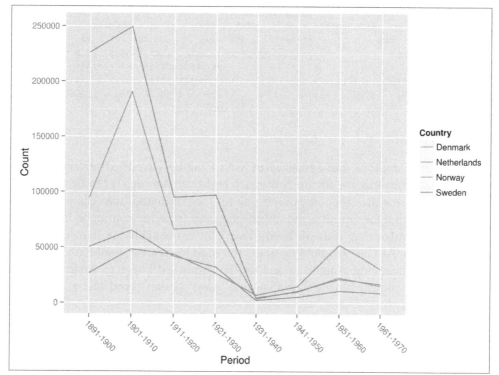

Figure 7-8. Line graph

```
$ < data/immigration.csv csvcut -c Period,Denmark,Netherlands,Norway,Sweden |
> header -d | tr , ' ' | feedgnuplot --terminal 'dumb 80,25' --lines \
> --autolegend --domain --legend 0 "Denmark" --legend 1 "Netherlands" \
> --legend 2 "Norway" --legend 3 "Sweden" --xlabel "Period" --unset grid --exit
```

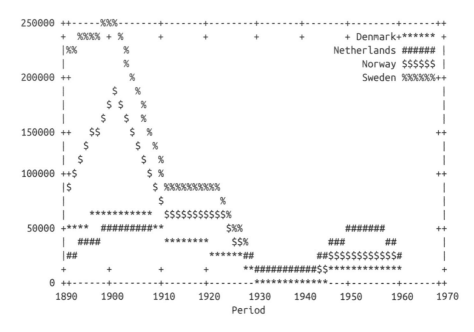

Summary

Both Rio with ggplot2 and feedgnuplot with Gnuplot have their advantages. The
plots generated by Rio are obviously of much higher quality. ggplot2 offers a consistent and concise syntax that lends itself well for the command line. The only down-
side would be that the output is not directly viewable from the command line. This is
where feedgnuplot may come in handy. Each plot has roughly the same command-
line arguments. As such, it would be straightforward to create a small Bash script that
would make generating plots from and for the command line even easier. After all,
with the command line having such a low resolution, we don't need a lot of flexibility.

Further Reading

- Wickham, H. (2009). *ggplot2: Elegant Graphics for Data Analysis*. Springer.
- Janert, P. K. (2009). *Gnuplot in Action*. Manning Publications.
- Tukey, J. W. (1977). *Exploratory Data Analysis*. Pearson.

Parallel Pipelines

In the previous chapters, we've been dealing with commands and pipelines that take care of an entire task at once. In practice, however, you may find yourself facing a task that requires the same command or pipeline to run multiple times. For, example, you may need to:

- Scrape hundreds of web pages
- Make dozens of API calls and transform their output
- Train a classifier for a range of parameter values
- Generate scatter plots for every pair of features in your data set

In any of these examples, there is a certain form of repetition involved. With your favorite scripting or programming language, you take care of this with a for loop or a while loop. On the command line, the first thing you might be inclined to do is to press **<Up>** (which brings back the previous command), modify the command if necessary, and press **<Enter>** (which runs the command again). This is fine for two or three times, but imagine doing this for, say, dozens of files. Such an approach quickly becomes cumbersome and inefficient. The good news is that we can write for and while loops on the command line as well.

Sometimes, repeating fast commands one after another (in serial) is sufficient. When you have multiple cores (and perhaps even multiple machines) it would be nice if you could make use of those, especially when you're faced with a data-intensive task. When using multiple cores or machines, the total running time may be reduced significantly. In this chapter, we'll introduce a very powerful tool called GNU Parallel that can take care of exactly this. GNU Parallel allows us to apply a command or pipeline with a range of arguments such as numbers, lines, and files. Plus, it allows us to run our commands in parallel.

Overview

This intermezzo chapter discusses several approaches to speed up tasks that require commands and pipelines to be run many times. The main goal of this chapter is to demonstrate to you the flexibility and power of a tool called GNU Parallel. Because this tool can be combined with any other tool discussed in this book, it will positively change the way you use the command line for data science. In this chapter, you'll learn about:

- Running commands in serial to a range of numbers, lines, and files
- Running pipelines in parallel using GNU Parallel
- Distributing pipelines on multiple machines

Serial Processing

Before we dive into parallelization, we'll look at looping in a serial fashion. It's worthwhile to know how to do this because this functionality is always available, the syntax closely resembles looping in other programming languages, and it will really make you appreciate the tool GNU Parallel.

From the examples provided in the introduction of this chapter, we can distill three types of items to loop over: numbers, lines, and files. These three types of items will be discussed in the next three subsections, respectively.

Looping Over Numbers

Imagine that we need to compute the square of every even integer between 0 and 100. There's a tool called bc, which is basically a calculator on the command line where you can pipe an equation to. The command to compute the square of 4 looks as follows:

```
$ echo "4^2" | bc
16
```

For a one-off calculation, this is perfect. However, as mentioned in the introduction, we would be crazy to press **<Up>**, change the number, and press **<Enter>** 51 times! In this case, it's better to let Bash do the hard work for us by using a for loop:

```
$ for i in {0..100..2}     ❶
> do
> echo "$i^2" | bc         ❷
> done | tail              ❸
6724
7056
7396
7744
8100
```

```
8464
8836
9216
9604
10000
```

There are a number of things going on here:

 Bash has a feature called brace expansion, which transforms {0..100..2} into a list separated by spaces: 0 2 4 ... 98 100.

 The variable i is assigned the value 1 in the first iteration, 2 in the second iteration, and so forth. The value of this variable can be employed in commands by prefixing it with a dollar sign ($). The shell will replace $i with its value before echo is executed. Note that there can be more than one command between do and done.

❸ We pipe the output of the for loop to tail so that we see the last ten values, only.

Although the syntax may appear a bit odd compared to your favorite programming language, it's worth remembering this because it's always available in the Bash shell. We'll shortly introduce a better and more flexible way of repeating commands.

Looping Over Lines

The second type of items we can loop over are lines. These lines can come from either a file or from standard input. This is a very generic approach because the lines can contain anything, including numbers, dates, and email addresses.

Imagine that we want to send an email to our customers. Let's generate some fake users using the Random User Generator API (*http://randomuser.me*):

```
$ cd ~/book/ch08
$ curl -s "http://api.randomuser.me/?results=5" > data/users.json
$ < data/users.json jq -r '.results[].user.email' > data/emails.txt
$ cat data/emails.txt
kaylee.anderson64@example.com
arthur.baker92@example.com
chloe.graham66@example.com
wyatt.nelson80@example.com
peter.coleman75@example.com
```

We can loop over the lines from *emails.txt* with a while loop:

```
$ while read line                                          ❶
> do
> echo "Sending invitation to ${line}."                    ❷
> done < data/emails.txt                                   ❸
Sending invitation to kaylee.anderson64@example.com.
Sending invitation to arthur.baker92@example.com.
```

```
Sending invitation to chloe.graham66@example.com.
Sending invitation to wyatt.nelson80@example.com.
Sending invitation to peter.coleman75@example.com.
```

 In this case we need to use a `while` loop because Bash does not know beforehand how many lines the input consists of.

 Although the curly braces around the `line` variable are not necessary in this case (because variable names cannot contain periods), it's still good practice.

❸ This redirection can also be placed before `while`.

You can also provide input to the `while` loop interactively by specifying the special file standard input */dev/stdin*. Press **<Ctrl-D>** when you're done:

```
$ while read i; do echo "You typed: $i."; done < /dev/stdin
one
You typed: one.
two
You typed: two.
three
You typed: three.
```

This method, however, has the disadvantage that, once you press **<Enter>**, the command(s) between do and done are run immediately for that line of input.

Looping Over Files

In this section, we discuss the third type of item that we often need to loop over: files. To handle special characters, use *globbing* (i.e., pathname expansion) instead of `ls`:

```
$ for filename in *.csv
> do
> echo "Processing ${filename}."
> done
Processing countries.csv.
```

Just as with brace expansion with numbers, the `*.csv` is first expanded into a list before it is processed by the `for` loop. A more elaborate alternative to finding files is `find` (Youngman, 2008), which:

- Allows for elaborate searching on properties such as size, access time, and permissions
- Handles dashes
- Handles special characters such as spaces and newlines

```
$ find data -name '*.csv' -exec echo "Processing {}" \;
Processing data/countries.csv
```

```
Processing data/movies.csv
Processing data/top250.csv
```

Here's the same example, but now using `parallel`:

```
$ find data -name '*.csv' -print0 | parallel -0 echo "Processing {}"
Processing data/countries.csv
Processing data/movies.csv
Processing data/top250.csv
```

The `-print0` option allows filenames that contain newlines or other types of white-space to be correctly interpreted by programs that process the output of `find`. If you are absolutely certain that the filenames contain no special characters such as spaces and newlines, then you can omit the `-print0` and `-0` options.

 If the list to process becomes too complex, you can always store the result to a temporary file and then use the method to loop over lines from a file.

Parallel Processing

Assume that we have a very long-running command, such as the one shown in Example 8-1.

Example 8-1. ~/book/ch08/slow.sh

```
#!/bin/bash
echo "Starting job $1"
duration=$((1+RANDOM%5))              ❶
sleep $duration
echo "Job $1 took ${duration} seconds"
```

❶ $RANDOM is an internal Bash function that returns a pseudorandom integer between 0 and 32,767. Taking the remainder of the division of that number by 5 and adding 1 ensures that the number is between 1 and 5.

This process does not take up all the resources we have available. And it so happens that we need to run this command a lot of times. For example, we need to download a long sequence of files.

A naive way to parallelize is to run the commands in the background:

```
$ for i in {1..4}; do
> (./slow.sh $i; echo Processed $i) &    ❶
> done
[1] 3334
[2] 3335
```

```
[3] 3336
[4] 3338
Starting job 2
Starting job 1
Starting job 3
Starting job 4
Job 4 took 1 seconds
Processed 4
Job 3 took 4 seconds
Job 2 took 4 seconds
Processed 3
Processed 2
Job 1 took 4 seconds
Processed 1
```

❶ Parentheses create a subshell. The ampersand (&) ensures that it will be executed in the background.

The problem with subshells is that they are executed all at once. There is no mechanism to control the maximum number of processes. You are not advised to use this:

```
$ while read i; do
> (./slow.sh "$i"; ) &
> done < data/movies.txt
[1] 3404
[2] 3405
[3] 3406
Starting job Star Wars
Starting job Matrix
Starting job Home Alone
[4] 3407
[5] 3410
Starting job Back to the Future
Starting job Indiana Jones
Job Home Alone took 2 seconds
Job Matrix took 2 seconds
Job Star Wars took 2 seconds
Job Back to the Future took 3 seconds
Job Indiana Jones took 4 seconds
```

Not everything can be parallelized: API calls may be limited to a certain number, or some commands can only have one instance.

Quoting is important. If we did not quote $i, then only the first word of each movie would have been passed to the script *slow.sh*.

There are two problems with this naive approach. First, there's no way to control how many processes you are running concurrently. The second issue is logging; which output belongs to which input:

Introducing GNU Parallel

GNU Parallel (Tange, 2014) is a command-line tool that allows us to parallelize commands and pipelines. The beauty of this tool is that existing tools can be used as they are; they do not need to be modified. Before we go into the details of GNU Parallel, here's a little teaser to show you how easy it is to parallelize the for loop stated above:

```
$ seq 5 | parallel "echo {}^2 | bc"
1
4
9
16
25
```

This is parallel in its simplest form: without any options. As you can see, it basically acts as a for loop. (We'll explain later what is going on exactly.) With no less than 110 options(!), GNU Parallel offers a lot of additional functionality. Don't worry, by the end of this chapter, you'll have a solid understanding of the most important ones.

Install GNU Parallel by running the following commands:

```
$ wget http://ftp.gnu.org/gnu/parallel/parallel-latest.tar.bz2
$ tar -xvjf parallel-latest.tar.bz2 > extracted-files
$ cd $(head -n 1 extracted-files)
$ ./configure && make && sudo make install
```

You may have noticed that we keep writing GNU Parallel. That's because there are two tools with the name "parallel." If you make use of the Data Science Toolbox you already have the correct one installed. Otherwise, double check that you have installed the correct tool installed by running parallel --version.

You can verify that you have correctly installed GNU Parallel:

```
$ parallel --version | head -n 1
GNU parallel 20140622
```

To delete the created files and directories, run the following:

```
$ cd ..
$ rm -r $(head -n 1 extracted-files)
$ rm parallel-latest.tar.bz2 extracted-files
```

If you use parallel as often as us then you may want to create an alias (e.g., p) by adding alias p=parallel to your ~/.bashrc. (In this chapter, we'll just use parallel for clarity.)

Specifying Input

The most important argument to GNU Parallel is the command that you would like to run for every input. The question is: where should the input item be inserted in the command line? If you do not specify anything, the input item will be appended to the command. While this is usually what you want, it's best to be explicit about where the input item should be inserted in the command using one or more placeholders.

 There are many ways to provide input to GNU Parallel. We prefer piping the input (as we do throughout this chapter) because that is generally applicable and allows us to construct a pipeline from left to right. Consult the man page of parallel to read about other ways to provide input.

In most cases, you probably want to use the entire input item as it is. For this, you only need one placeholder. You specify the placeholder with two curly braces ({}):

```
$ seq 5 | parallel echo {}
```

When the input item is a file, there are a couple of special placeholders you can use to modify the filename. For example, with {./}, only the basename of the filename will be used.

If the input line has multiple parts separated by a delimiter, you can add numbers to the placeholders. For example:

```
$ < input.csv parallel -C, "mv {1} {2}"
```

Here, you can apply the same placeholder modifiers. It's also possible to reuse the same input item. If the input to parallel is a CSV file with a header, then you can use the column names as placeholders:

```
$ < input.csv parallel -C, --header : "invite {name} {email}"
```

Sometimes you just want to run the same command without any changing inputs. This is also possible in parallel. We just have to specify the -N0 option and give as input as many lines as you want to execute:

```
$ seq 5 | parallel -N0 "echo The command line rules"
The command line rules
The command line rules
The command line rules
```

The command line rules

 If you ever wonder whether your GNU Parallel command is set up correctly, you can add the --dryrun option. Instead of actually executing the command, GNU Parallel will print out all the commands exactly as if they would have been executed.

Controlling the Number of Concurrent Jobs

By default, `parallel` runs one job per CPU core in parallel. You can control the number of jobs that will be run in parallel with the --jobs or -j option. Simply specifying a number, say n, means that n jobs will be run in parallel. If you put a plus sign in front of the number n, then `parallel` will run $m+n$ jobs plus the number of CPU cores, where m is the number of CPU cores. If you put a minus sign in front of the number, then `parallel` will run $m-n$ jobs. You can also specify a percentage to the -j option. So, the default is 100% of the number of CPU cores. The optimal number of jobs to run in parallel depends on the actual commands you are running:

```
$ seq 5 | parallel -j0 "echo Hi {}"
Hi 1
Hi 2
Hi 3
Hi 4
Hi 5

$ seq 5 | parallel -j200% "echo Hi {}"
Hi 1
Hi 2
Hi 3
Hi 4
Hi 5
```

If you specify -j1, then the commands will be run in serial. Even though this doesn't do the name of the tool of justice, it still has its uses. For example, when you need to access an API which only allows one connection at a time. If you specify -j0, then `parallel` will run as many jobs in parallel as possible. This can be compared to looping with subshells, which is not advised.

Logging and Output

To save the output of each command, you might be tempted to do the following:

```
$ seq 5 | parallel "echo \"Hi {}\" > data/hi-{}.txt"
```

This will save the output into individual files. Or, if you want to save everything into one big file, you could do the following:

```
$ seq 5 | parallel "echo Hi {}" >> data/one-big-file.txt
```

However, GNU Parallel offers the --results option, which stores the output of each job into a separate file, where the filename is based on the input values:

```
$ seq 5 | parallel --results data/outdir "echo Hi {}"
Hi 1
Hi 2
Hi 3
Hi 4
Hi 5
$ find data/outdir
data/outdir
data/outdir/1
data/outdir/1/1
data/outdir/1/1/stderr
data/outdir/1/1/stdout
data/outdir/1/3
data/outdir/1/3/stderr
data/outdir/1/3/stdout
data/outdir/1/5
data/outdir/1/5/stderr
data/outdir/1/5/stdout
data/outdir/1/2
data/outdir/1/2/stderr
data/outdir/1/2/stdout
data/outdir/1/4
data/outdir/1/4/stderr
data/outdir/1/4/stdout
```

When you're running multiple jobs in parallel, the order in which the jobs are run may not correspond to the order of the input. The output of jobs is therefore also mixed up. To keep the same order, simply specify the --keep-order or -k option.

Sometimes it's useful to record which input generated which output. GNU Parallel allows you to *tag* the output with the --tag option:

```
$ seq 5 | parallel --tag "echo Hi {}"
1       Hi 1
2       Hi 2
3       Hi 3
4       Hi 4
5       Hi 5
```

Creating Parallel Tools

The bc tool, which we used in the beginning of the chapter, is not parallel by itself. However, we can parallelize it using parallel. The Data Science Toolbox contains a tool called pbc (Janssens, 2014). Its source code is shown in Example 8-2.

Example 8-2. Parallel bc (pbc)

```bash
#!/usr/bin/env bash
parallel -C, -k -j100% "echo '$1' | bc -l"
```

This tool allows us to simplify the code used in the beginning of the chapter, too:

```
$ seq 100 | pbc '{1}^2' | tail
8281
8464
8649
8836
9025
9216
9409
9604
9801
10000
```

This tool works as follows. You may remember that `seq 100` generates integers 1 to 100, one per line. These lines get piped to `pbc`, which, in turn, feeds them to `paral lel`. The argument to `{1}` is evaluated by `parallel` before it sends it to `bc`. This means that `{1}` gets replaced by the value of the first column (there is only one column) on the line in question.

Distributed Processing

Sometimes you need more power than your local machine, even with all its cores, can offer. Luckily, GNU Parallel can also leverage the power of remote machines, which really allows us to speed up our pipeline.

What's great is that GNU Parallel does not have to be installed on the remote machine. All that's required is that you can connect to the remote machine via SSH, which is also what GNU Parallel uses to distribute our pipeline. (Having GNU Parallel installed remotely is helpful because it can then determine how many cores to employ on each remote machine; more on this later.)

First, we're going to obtain a list of running AWS EC2 instances. Don't worry if you don't have any remote machines, you can replace any occurrence of `--slf instan ces`, which tells GNU Parallel which remote machines to use, with `--sshlogin :`. This way, you can still follow along with the examples in this section.

Once we know which remote machines to take over, we're going to consider three flavors of distributed processing:

- Running ordinary commands on remote machines
- Distributing local data directly among remote machines
- Sending files to remote machines, processing them, and retrieving the results

Get a List of Running AWS EC2 Instances

In this section, we're creating a file named *instances* that will contain one hostname of a remote machine per line. We're using Amazon Web Services in this section. If you're using a different cloud computing service, or have your own servers, make sure that you create an *instances* file yourself.

We can obtain a list of running AWS EC2 instances from the command line using aws, the command-line interface to the AWS API (Amazon Web Services, 2014). If you're not using the Data Science Toolbox, install awscli using pip (PyPA, 2014) as follows:

```
$ pip install awscli
```

With aws, you can virtually do everything you can do with the online AWS Management Console. We just use this tool to obtain a list of running EC2 instances from AWS, but it can do a lot more. We assume that you know how to launch instances, either through the online AWS Management Console or through the aws command-line tool.

The command aws ec2 describe-instances returns a lot of information about all your EC2 instances in JSON format (see the AWS documentation (*http://bit.ly/aws_docs*). We extract the relevant fields using jq:

```
$ aws ec2 describe-instances | jq '.Reservations[].Instances[] | '\
> '{public_dns: .PublicDnsName, state: .State.Name}'
{
  "state": "running",
  "public_dns": "ec2-54-88-122-140.compute-1.amazonaws.com"
}
{
  "state": "stopped",
  "public_dns": null
}
```

The possible states of an EC2 instance are *pending, running, shutting-down, terminated, stopping,* and *stopped*. Because we can only distribute our pipeline to running instances, we filter out the nonrunning instances:

```
$ aws ec2 describe-instances | jq -r '.Reservations[].Instances[] | '\
> 'select(.State.Name=="running") | .PublicDnsName' > instances
$ cat instances
```

```
ec2-54-88-122-140.compute-1.amazonaws.com
ec2-54-88-89-208.compute-1.amazonaws.com
```

(If we would leave out -r, which stands for *raw*, the hostnames would have been surrounded by double quotes.) We save the output to *instances*, so that we can pass this to `parallel` later.

As mentioned, `parallel` employs SSH to connect to the EC2 instances. Add the following to *~/.ssh/config*, so that SSH knows how to connect to the EC2 instances:

```
Host *.amazonaws.com
    IdentityFile ~/.ssh/MyKeyFile.pem
    User ubuntu
```

Depending on which distribution you're running, your username may be different than ubuntu.

Running Commands on Remote Machines

The first flavor of distributed processing is to simply run ordinary commands on remote machines. Let's first double-check that `parallel` is working by running the command-line tool `hostname` to get a list of hosts:

```
$ parallel --nonall --slf instances hostname
ip-172-31-23-204
ip-172-31-23-205
```

Here, the --slf option is short for the --sshloginfile option. The --nonall option instructs `parallel` to execute the same command on every remote machine in the *instances* file without using any parameters. Remember, if you don't have any remote machines to utilize, you can replace --slf instances with --sshlogin : so that the command runs on your local machine:

```
$ parallel --nonall --sshlogin : hostname
data-science-toolbox
```

Running the same command on every remote machine once only requires one CPU core per machine. If we wanted to distribute the list of arguments passed in to `parallel` then it could potentially use more than one CPU core. If the number of CPU cores is not specified explicitly, `parallel` will try to determine this:

```
$ seq 2 | parallel --slf instances echo 2>&1 | fold
bash: parallel: command not found
parallel: Warning: Could not figure out number of cpus on ec2-54-88-122-140.comp
ute-1.amazonaws.com (). Using 1.
1
2
```

In this case, we have `parallel` installed on one of the two remote machines. We're getting a warning message indicating that `parallel` is not found on one of them. As a result, `parallel` cannot determine the number of cores and will default to using one CPU core. When you receive this warning message, you can do one of the following four things:

- Don't worry, and be happy with using one CPU core per machine.
- Specify the number of jobs per machine via the `-j` option.
- Specify the number of cores to use per machine by putting, for example, 2/ if you want two cores, in front of each hostname in the *instances* file.
- Install GNU Parallel using a package manager (not that this is usually not the latest version). For example, on Ubuntu:

```
$ parallel --nonall --slf instances "sudo apt-get install -y parallel"
```

Distributing Local Data Among Remote Machines

The second flavor of distributed processing is to distribute local data directly among remote machines. Imagine you have one very large data set that you want to process using multiple remote machines. For simplicity, we're going to sum all integers from 1 to 1,000. First, let's verify that our input is actually being distributed by printing the hostname of the remote machine and the length of the input it received using `wc`:

```
$ seq 1000 | parallel -N100 --pipe --slf hosts  "(hostname; wc -l) | paste -sd:"
ip-172-31-23-204:100
ip-172-31-23-205:100
ip-172-31-23-205:100
ip-172-31-23-204:100
ip-172-31-23-205:100
ip-172-31-23-204:100
ip-172-31-23-205:100
ip-172-31-23-204:100
ip-172-31-23-205:100
ip-172-31-23-204:100
```

We can verify that our 1,000 numbers get distributed evenly in subsets of 100 (as specified by `-N100`). Now, we're ready to sum all those numbers:

```
$ seq 1000 | parallel -N100 --pipe --slf hosts "paste -sd+ | bc" |
> paste -sd+ | bc
500500
```

Here, we immediately also sum the 10 sums we get back from the remote machines. Let's double check the answer is correct:

```
$ seq 1000 | paste -sd+ | bc
500500
```

Good, that works. If you have a larger command that you want to execute on the remote machines, you can also put it in a separate script and upload it with `parallel`. In our case, let's create a simple command-line tool called *sum*:

```
#!/usr/bin/env bash
paste -sd+ | bc
```

Don't forget to make it executable as discussed in Chapter 4. The following command first uploads the file *sum*:

```
$ seq 1000 | parallel -N100 --basefile sum --pipe --slf instances './sum' |
> ./sum
500500
```

Of course, summing 1,000 numbers is only a toy example. It would have been much faster to do this locally. However, we hope it's clear from this toy example that GNU Parallel can be incredibly powerful.

Processing Files on Remote Machines

The third flavor of distributed processing is to send files to remote machines, process them, and retrieve the results. Imagine that we want to count for each borough of New York City, how often they receive service calls on 311. We don't have that data on our local machine yet, so let's first obtain it from NYC Open Data (*https://data.cityof newyork.us*) using its great API:

```
$ seq 0 100 900 | parallel  "curl -sL 'http://data.cityofnewyork.us/resource'"\
> "'/erm2-nwe9.json?\$limit=100&\$offset={}' | jq -c '.[]' | gzip > {#}.json.gz"
```

Note that `jq -c '.[]'` is used to flatten the array of JSON objects so that there's one line per object. We now have 10 files containing compressed JSON data. Let's see what one line of JSON looks like:

```
$ zcat 1.json.gz | head -n 1 | fold
{"school_region":"Unspecified","park_facility_name":"Unspecified","x_coordinate_
state_plane":"945974","agency_name":"Department of Health and Mental Hygiene","u
nique_key":"147","facility_type":"N/A","status":"Assigned","school_address":"Uns
pecified","created_date":"2006-08-29T21:25:23","community_board":"01 STATEN ISLA
ND","incident_zip":"10302","school_name":"Unspecified","location":{"latitude":"4
0.62745427115626","longitude":"-74.13789056665027","needs_recoding":false},"comp
laint_type":"Food Establishment","city":"STATEN ISLAND","park_borough":"STATEN I
SLAND","school_state":"Unspecified","longitude":"-74.13789056665027","intersecti
on_street_1":"DECKER AVENUE","y_coordinate_state_plane":"167905","due_date":"200
6-10-05T21:25:23","latitude":"40.62745427115626","school_code":"Unspecified","sc
hool_city":"Unspecified","address_type":"INTERSECTION","intersection_street_2":"
BARRETT AVENUE","school_number":"Unspecified","resolution_action_updated_date":"
2006-10-06T00:00:17","descriptor":"Handwashing","school_zip":"Unspecified","loca
tion_type":"Restaurant/Bar/Deli/Bakery","agency":"DOHMH","borough":"STATEN ISLAN
D","school_phone_number":"Unspecified"}
```

If we were to get the total number of service calls per borough on our local machine, we would run the following command:

```
$ zcat *.json.gz |                    ❶
> jq -r '.borough' |                  ❷
> tr '[A-Z] ' '[a-z]_' |             ❸
> sort | uniq -c |                    ❹
> awk '{print $2","$1}' |             ❺
> header -a borough,count |           ❻
> csvsort -rc count | csvlook         ❼
|----------------+--------|
|   borough      | count  |
|----------------+--------|
|   unspecified  | 467    |
|   manhattan    | 274    |
|   brooklyn     | 103    |
|   queens       | 77     |
|   bronx        | 44     |
|   staten_island| 35     |
|----------------+--------|
```

Because this is quite a long pipeline, and because we're using it again in a moment with `parallel`, it's worth reviewing:

❶ Expand all compressed files using `zcat`

❷ For each call, extract the name of the borough using `jq`

❸ Convert borough names to lowercase and replace spaces with underscores (because `awk` splits on whitespace by default)

❹ Count the occurrences of each borough using `sort` and `uniq`

❺ Reverse the fields `count` and `borough` and make it comma delimited using `awk`

❻ Add a header using `header`

❼ Sort by `count` using `csvsort` (Groskopf, 2014) and print a table using `csvlook`

Imagine, for a moment, that our own machine is so slow that we simply cannot perform this pipeline locally. We can use GNU Parallel to distribute the local files among the remote machines, let them do the processing, and retrieve the results:

```
$ ls *.json.gz |                                                    ❶
> parallel -v --basefile jq \                                       ❷
> --trc {.}.csv \                                                   ❸
> --slf instances \                                                 ❹
> "zcat {} | ./jq -r '.borough' | tr '[A-Z] ' '[a-z]_' | sort | uniq -c |"\
> " awk '{print \$2\",\"\$1}' > {.}.csv"                            ❺
```

```
zcat 10.json.gz | ./jq -r '.borough' | sort | uniq -c | awk '{print $2","$1}'
zcat 2.json.gz | ./jq -r '.borough' | sort | uniq -c | awk '{print $2","$1}'
zcat 1.json.gz | ./jq -r '.borough' | sort | uniq -c | awk '{print $2","$1}'
zcat 3.json.gz | ./jq -r '.borough' | sort | uniq -c | awk '{print $2","$1}'
zcat 4.json.gz | ./jq -r '.borough' | sort | uniq -c | awk '{print $2","$1}'
zcat 5.json.gz | ./jq -r '.borough' | sort | uniq -c | awk '{print $2","$1}'
zcat 6.json.gz | ./jq -r '.borough' | sort | uniq -c | awk '{print $2","$1}'
zcat 7.json.gz | ./jq -r '.borough' | sort | uniq -c | awk '{print $2","$1}'
zcat 8.json.gz | ./jq -r '.borough' | sort | uniq -c | awk '{print $2","$1}'
zcat 9.json.gz | ./jq -r '.borough' | sort | uniq -c | awk '{print $2","$1}'
```

This long command breaks down as follows:

❶ Print the list of files using ls and pipe it into parallel.

❷ Transmit the jq binary to each remote machine. (Luckily, jq has no dependencies.) This file will be removed from the remote machine at the end because we specified the --trc option (which implies the --cleanup option).

❸ The --trc {.}.csv option is short for --transfer --return {.}.csv --cleanup. (The replacement string {.} gets replaced with the input filename without the last extension.) Here, this means that the JSON file gets transferred to the remote machine, the CSV file gets returned to the local machine, and both files will be removed from the remote machine after each job.

❹ Specify a list of hostnames. Remember, if you want to try this out locally, you can specify --sshlogin : instead of --self instances.

❺ Note the escaping in the awk expression. Quoting can sometimes be tricky. Here, the dollar signs and the double quotes are escaped. If quoting ever gets too confusing, remember that you can put turn pipeline into a separate command-line tool just as we did with sum.

If we, at some point during this command, run ls on one of the remote machines, we would see that parallel indeed transfers (and cleans up) the binary jq, the JSON files, and CSV files:

```
$ ssh $(head -n 1 instances) ls
1.json.csv
1.json.gz
jq
```

Each CSV file looks like this:

```
$ cat 1.json.csv
bronx,3
brooklyn,5
manhattan,24
queens,3
```

```
staten_island,2
unspecified,63
```

We can sum the counts in each CSV file using Rio and the aggregate function in R:

```
$ cat *.csv | header -a borough,count |
> Rio -e 'aggregate(count ~ borough, df, sum)' |
> csvsort -rc count | csvlook
|-----------------+--------|
| borough         | count  |
|-----------------+--------|
| unspecified     | 467    |
| manhattan       | 274    |
| brooklyn        | 103    |
| queens          | 77     |
| bronx           | 44     |
| staten_island   | 35     |
|-----------------+--------|
```

Or, if you prefer to use SQL to aggregate results, you can use csvsql as discussed in Chapter 5:

```
$ cat *.csv | header -a borough,count |
> csvsql --query 'SELECT borough, SUM(count) AS count FROM stdin '\
> 'GROUP BY borough ORDER BY count DESC' | csvlook
|-----------------+--------|
| borough         | count  |
|-----------------+--------|
| unspecified     | 467    |
| manhattan       | 274    |
| brooklyn        | 103    |
| queens          | 77     |
| bronx           | 44     |
| staten_island   | 35     |
|-----------------+--------|
```

Discussion

As data scientists, we work with data, and sometimes a lot of data. This means that we often need to run a command multiple times or distribute data-intensive commands over multiple CPU cores or machines. This chapter has shown how easy it is to parallelize commands. GNU Parallel is a very powerful and flexible tool to speed up ordinary command-line tools and distribute them over multiple cores and remote machines. It offers a lot of functionality, and in this chapter we've only been able to scratch the surface. Some features of GNU Parallel that we haven't covered include:

- Keep a log of all the jobs
- Only start new jobs when the load of a machine is beneath a certain threshold
- Time out, resume, and retry jobs

Once you have a basic understanding of GNU Parallel and its most important options, we recommend that you take a look at its tutorial listed in the Further Reading section.

Further Reading

- Tange, O. (2011). GNU Parallel—The Command-Line Power Tool." *;Login: The USENIX Magazine, 36*(1), 42–47. Retrieved from *http://www.gnu.org/s/parallel.*
- Tange, O. (2014). GNU Parallel Tutorial. Retrieved from *http://www.gnu.org/soft ware/parallel/parallel_tutorial.html.*
- Amazon Web Services (2014). AWS Command Line Interface Documentation. Retrieved from *http://aws.amazon.com/documentation/cli/.*

Modeling Data

In this chapter, we'll perform the fourth step of the OSEMN model (and the last step to require a computer): modeling data. Generally speaking, to model data is to create an abstract or higher-level description of your data. Just like with creating visualizations, it's like taking a step back from the individual data points.

Visualizations, on the one hand, are characterized by shapes, positions, and colors such that we can interpret them by looking at them. Models, on the other hand, are internally characterized by a bunch of numbers, which means that computers can use them, for example, to make predictions about new data points. (We can still visualize models so that we can try to understand them and see how they are performing.)

In this chapter, we'll consider four common types of algorithms to model data:

- Dimensionality reduction
- Clustering
- Regression
- Classification

These four types of algorithms come from the field of machine learning. As such, we're going to change our vocabulary a bit. Let's assume that we have a CSV file, also known as a *data set*. Each row, except for the header, is considered to be a *data point*. For simplicity we assume that each column that contains numerical values is an input *feature*. If a data point also contains a nonnumerical field, such as the *species* column in the Iris data set, then that is known as the data point's *label*.

The first two types of algorithms (dimensionality reduction and clustering) are most often unsupervised, which means that they create a model based on the features of the data set only. The last two types of algorithms (regression and classification) are by definition supervised algorithms, which means that they also incorporate the labels into the model.

 This is by no means an introduction to machine learning. That implies that we must skim over many details. We strongly advise that you become familiar with an algorithm before applying it blindly to your data.

Overview

In this chapter, you'll learn how to:

- Reduce the dimensionality of your data set
- Identify groups of data points with three clustering algorithms
- Predict the quality of white wine using regression
- Classify wine as red or white via a prediction API

More Wine, Please!

In this chapter, we'll use a data set of wine tastings—specifically, red and white Portuguese Vinho Verde wine. Each data point represents a wine, and consists of 11 physicochemical properties: (1) fixed acidity, (2) volatile acidity, (3) citric acid, (4) residual sugar, (5) chlorides, (6) free sulfur dioxide, (7) total sulfur dioxide, (8) density, (9) pH, (10) sulphates, and (11) alcohol. There is also a quality score. This score lies between 0 (very bad) and 10 (excellent) and is the median of at least three evaluations by wine experts. More information about this data set is available at the Wine Quality Data Set web page (*http://archive.ics.uci.edu/ml/datasets/Wine+Quality*).

There are two data sets: one for white wine and one for red wine. The very first step is to obtain the two data sets using curl (and of course parallel because we haven't got all day):

```
$ cd ~/book/ch09/data
$ parallel "curl -sL http://archive.ics.uci.edu/ml/machine-learning-databases"\
> "/wine-quality/winequality-{}.csv > wine-{}.csv" ::: red white
```

(The triple colon is another way to pass data to parallel.) Let's inspect both data sets using head and count the number of rows using wc -l:

```
$ head -n 5 wine-{red,white}.csv | fold
==> wine-red.csv <==
"fixed acidity";"volatile acidity";"citric acid";"residual sugar";"chlorides";"f
ree sulfur dioxide";"total sulfur dioxide";"density";"pH";"sulphates";"alcohol";
"quality"
```

```
7.4;0.7;0;1.9;0.076;11;34;0.9978;3.51;0.56;9.4;5
7.8;0.88;0;2.6;0.098;25;67;0.9968;3.2;0.68;9.8;5
7.8;0.76;0.04;2.3;0.092;15;54;0.997;3.26;0.65;9.8;5
11.2;0.28;0.56;1.9;0.075;17;60;0.998;3.16;0.58;9.8;6

==> wine-white.csv <==
"fixed acidity";"volatile acidity";"citric acid";"residual sugar";"chlorides";"f
ree sulfur dioxide";"total sulfur dioxide";"density";"pH";"sulphates";"alcohol";
"quality"
7;0.27;0.36;20.7;0.045;45;170;1.001;3;0.45;8.8;6
6.3;0.3;0.34;1.6;0.049;14;132;0.994;3.3;0.49;9.5;6
8.1;0.28;0.4;6.9;0.05;30;97;0.9951;3.26;0.44;10.1;6
7.2;0.23;0.32;8.5;0.058;47;186;0.9956;3.19;0.4;9.9;6
$ wc -l wine-{red,white}.csv
  1600 wine-red.csv
  4899 wine-white.csv
  6499 total
```

At first sight this data appears to be very clean already. Still, let's scrub this data a little bit so that it conforms more with what most command-line tools are expecting. Specifically, we'll:

- Convert the header to lowercase
- Convert the semicolons to commas
- Convert spaces to underscores
- Remove unnecessary quotes

These things can all be taken care of by `tr`. Let's use a `for` loop this time—for old times' sake—to process both data sets:

```
$ for T in red white; do
> < wine-$T.csv tr '[A-Z]; ' '[a-z],_' | tr -d \" > wine-${T}-clean.csv
> done
```

Let's combine the two data sets. We'll use `csvstack` to add a column named `type` which will be `red` for rows of the first file, and `white` for rows of the second file:

```
$ HEADER="$(head -n 1 wine-red-clean.csv),type"
$ csvstack -g red,white -n type wine-{red,white}-clean.csv |
> csvcut -c $HEADER > wine-both-clean.csv
```

The new column `type` is added to the beginning of the table. Because some of the command-line tools that we'll use in this chapter assume that the class label is the last column, we'll rearrange the columns by using `csvcut`. Instead of typing all 13 columns, we temporarily store the desired header into a variable `HEADER` before we call `csvstack`.

It's good to check whether there are any missing values in this data set:

```
$ csvstat wine-both-clean.csv --nulls
  1. fixed_acidity: False
  2. volatile_acidity: False
  3. citric_acid: False
  4. residual_sugar: False
  5. chlorides: False
  6. free_sulfur_dioxide: False
  7. total_sulfur_dioxide: False
  8. density: False
  9. ph: False
 10. sulphates: False
 11. alcohol: False
 12. quality: False
 13. type: False
```

Excellent! Just out of curiosity, let's see what the distribution of quality looks like for both red and white wines:

```
$ < wine-both-clean.csv Rio -ge 'g+geom_density(aes(quality, '\
> 'fill=type), adjust=3, alpha=0.5)' | display
```

From the density plot shown in Figure 9-1, we can see the quality of white wine is distributed more towards higher values.

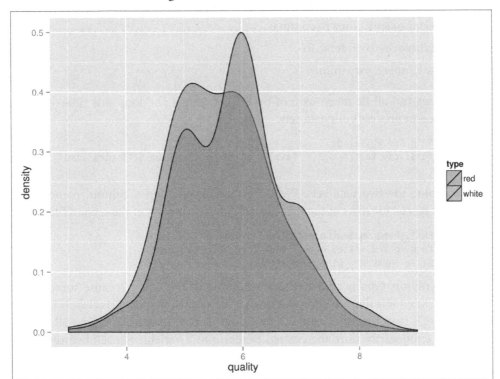

Figure 9-1. Comparing the quality of red and white wines using a density plot

Does this mean that white wines are overall better than red wines, or that the white wine experts more easily give higher scores than red wine experts? That's something that the data doesn't tell us. Or is there perhaps a correlation between alcohol and quality? Let's use Rio and ggplot2 again to find out (Figure 9-2):

```
$ < wine-both-clean.csv Rio -ge 'ggplot(df, aes(x=alcohol, y=quality, '\
> 'color=type)) + geom_point(position="jitter", alpha=0.2) + '\
> 'geom_smooth(method="lm")' | display
```

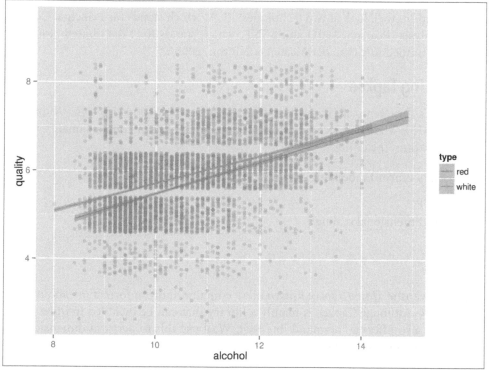

Figure 9-2. Correlation between the alcohol contents of wine and its quality

Eureka! Ahem, let's carry on with some modeling, shall we?

Dimensionality Reduction with Tapkee

The goal of dimensionality reduction is to map high-dimensional data points onto a lower dimensional space. The challenge is to keep similar data points close together on the lower-dimensional mapping. As we've seen in the previous section, our wine data set contains 13 features. We'll stick with two dimensions because that's straight-forward to visualize.

Dimensionality reduction is often regarded as being part of the exploring step. It's useful for when there are too many features for plotting. You could do a scatter plot matrix, but that only shows you two features at a time. It's also useful as a pre-processing step for other machine-learning algorithms.

Most dimensionality reduction algorithms are unsupervised. This means that they don't employ the labels of the data points in order to construct the lower-dimensional mapping.

In this section, we'll look at two techniques: PCA, which stands for Principal Components Analysis (Pearson, 1901) and t-SNE, which stands for t-distributed Stochastic Neighbor Embedding (van der Maaten & Hinton, 2008).

Introducing Tapkee

Tapkee is a C++ template library for dimensionality reduction (Lisitsyn, Widmer, & Garcia, 2013). The library contains implementations of many dimensionality reduction algorithms, including:

- Locally Linear Embedding
- Isomap
- Multidimensional scaling
- PCA
- t-SNE

Tapkee's website (*http://tapkee.lisitsyn.me/*) contains more information about these algorithms. Although Tapkee is mainly a library that can be included in other applications, it also offers a command-line tool. We'll use this to perform dimensionality reduction on our wine data set.

Installing Tapkee

If you aren't running the Data Science Toolbox, you'll need to download and compile Tapkee yourself. First make sure that you have CMake installed. On Ubuntu, you simply run:

```
$ sudo apt-get install cmake
```

Consult Tapkee's website for instructions for other operating systems. Then execute the following commands to download the source and compile it:

```
$ curl -sL https://github.com/lisitsyn/tapkee/archive/master.tar.gz > \
> tapkee-master.tar.gz
$ tar -xzf tapkee-master.tar.gz
$ cd tapkee-master
$ mkdir build && cd build
```

```
$ cmake ..
$ make
```

This creates a binary executable named `tapkee`.

Linear and Nonlinear Mappings

First, we'll scale the features using standardization such that each feature is equally important. This generally leads to better results when applying machine-learning algorithms.

To scale we use a combination of `cols` and `Rio`:

```
$ < wine-both.csv cols -C type Rio -f scale > wine-both-scaled.csv
```

Now we apply both dimensionality reduction techniques and visualize the mapping using `Rio-scatter` (Figure 9-3):

```
$ < wine-both-scaled.csv cols -C type,quality body tapkee --method pca |
> header -r x,y,type,quality | Rio-scatter x y type | display
```

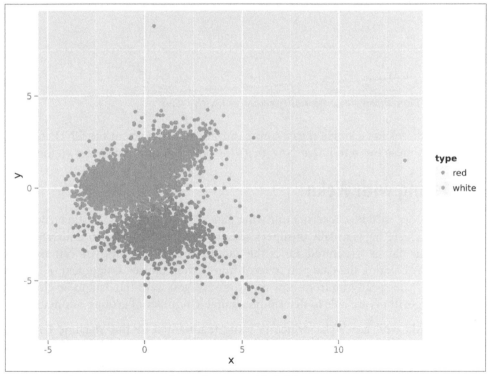

Figure 9-3. Linear dimensionality reduction with PCA

```
$ < wine-both-scaled.csv cols -C type,quality body tapkee --method t-sne |
> header -r x,y,type,quality | Rio-scatter x y type | display
```

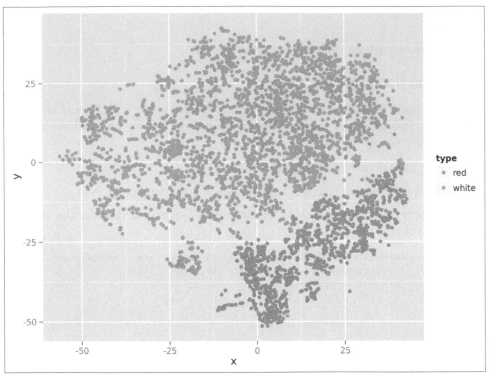

Figure 9-4. Non-linear dimensionality reduction with t-SNE

Note that there's not a single *classic* command-line tool (i.e., from the GNU coreutils package) in these two one-liners. Now that's the power of creating your own tools!

Clustering with Weka

In this section, we'll be clustering our wine data set into groups. Like dimensionality reduction, clustering is usually unsupervised. It can be used to gain an understanding of how your data is structured. Once the data has been clustered, you can visualize the result by coloring the data points according to their cluster assignment. For most algorithms, you specify up front how many groups you want the data to be clustered in; some algorithms are able to determine a suitable number of groups automatically.

For this task, we'll use Weka, which is being maintained by the Machine Learning Group at the University of Waikato (Hall et al., 2009). If you already know Weka, then you probably know it as a software with a graphical user interface. However, as you'll see, Weka can also be used from the command line (albeit with some modifications). Besides clustering, Weka can also do classification and regression, but we're going to be using other tools for those machine-learning tasks.

Introducing Weka

You may ask, surely there are better command-line tools for clustering? And you are right. One reason we include Weka in this chapter is to show you how you can work around imperfections by building additional command-line tools. As you spend more time on the command line and try out other command-line tools, chances are that you come across one that seems very promising at first, but does not work as you expected. A common imperfection, for example, is that the command-line tool does not handle standard input or standard output correctly. In the next section, we'll point out Weka's imperfections and demonstrate how we work around them.

Taming Weka on the Command Line

Weka can be invoked from the command line, but it's definitely not straightforward or user friendly. Weka is programmed in Java, which means that you have to run java, specify the location of the *weka.jar* file, and specify the individual class you want to call. For example, Weka has a class called *MexicanHat*, which generates a toy data set. To generate 10 data points using this class, you would run:

```
$ java -cp ~/bin/weka.jar weka.datagenerators.classifiers.regression.MexicanHat\
>  -n 10 | fold
%
% Commandline
%
% weka.datagenerators.classifiers.regression.MexicanHat -r weka.datagenerators.c
lassifiers.regression.MexicanHat-S_1_-n_10_-A_1.0_-R_-10..10_-N_0.0_-V_1.0 -S 1
-n 10 -A 1.0 -R -10..10 -N 0.0 -V 1.0
%
@relation weka.datagenerators.classifiers.regression.MexicanHat-S_1_-n_10_-A_1.0
_-R_-10..10_-N_0.0_-V_1.0

@attribute x numeric
@attribute y numeric

@data

4.617564,-0.215591
-1.798384,0.541716
-5.845703,-0.072474
-3.345659,-0.060572
9.355118,0.00744
-9.877656,-0.044298
9.274096,0.016186
8.797308,0.066736
8.943898,0.051718
8.741643,0.072209
```

Don't worry about the output of this command; we'll discuss that later. At this moment, we're concerned with the usage of Weka. There are three things to note here:

- We need to run `java`, which is counterintuitive.
- The JAR file contains over 2,000 classes, and only about 300 of those can be used from the command line directly. How do we know which ones?
- We need to specify the entire namespace of the class: `weka.datagenera tors.classifiers.regression.MexicanHat`. How are we supposed to remember that?

Does this mean that we're going to give up on Weka? Of course not! Weka contains a lot of useful functionality and we're going to tackle these three issues in the next three subsections.

An improved command-line tool for Weka

To address the first issue, save the following snippet as a new file called *weka*, make it executable, and move it to a directory that's on your PATH:

```
#!/usr/bin/env bash
java -Xmx1024M -cp ${WEKAPATH}/weka.jar "weka.$@"
```

Subsequently, add the following line to your *~/.bashrc* file so that weka can be called from anywhere:

```
$ export WEKAPATH=/home/vagrant/repos/weka
```

We can now call the previous example with:

```
$ weka datagenerators.classifiers.regression.MexicanHat -n 10
```

Now that's already an improvement!

Usable Weka classes

As mentioned, the file *weka.jar* contains over 2,000 classes. Many of them cannot be used from the command line directly. We consider a class usable from the command line when it provides us with a help message if we invoke it with the `-h` option. For example:

```
$ weka datagenerators.classifiers.regression.MexicanHat -h

Data Generator options:

-h
        Prints this help.
-o <file>
        The name of the output file, otherwise the generated data is
```

```
               printed to stdout.
 -r <name>
               The name of the relation.
 -d
               Whether to print debug informations.
 -S
               The seed for random function (default 1)
 -n <num>
               The number of examples to generate (default 100)
 -A <num>
               The amplitude multiplier (default 1.0).
 -R <num>..<num>
               The range x is randomly drawn from (default -10.0..10.0).
 -N <num>
               The noise rate (default 0.0).
 -V <num>
               The noise variance (default 1.0).
```

Now that's usable. The following class, for example, is not usable:

```
$ weka filters.SimpleFilter -h
java.lang.ClassNotFoundException: -h
        at java.net.URLClassLoader$1.run(URLClassLoader.java:202)
        at java.security.AccessController.doPrivileged(Native Method)
        at java.net.URLClassLoader.findClass(URLClassLoader.java:190)
        at java.lang.ClassLoader.loadClass(ClassLoader.java:306)
        at sun.misc.Launcher$AppClassLoader.loadClass(Launcher.java:301)
        at java.lang.ClassLoader.loadClass(ClassLoader.java:247)
        at java.lang.Class.forName0(Native Method)
        at java.lang.Class.forName(Class.java:171)
        at weka.filters.Filter.main(Filter.java:1344)
-h
```

The following pipeline runs weka with the -h option for every class in *weka.jar* and saves the standard output and standard error to a file with the same name as the class:

```
$ unzip -l $WEKAPATH/weka.jar |
> sed -rne 's/.*(weka)\/([^g])([^$]*)\.class$/\2\3/p' |
> tr '/' '.' |
> parallel --timeout 1 -j4 -v "weka {} -h > {} 2>&1"
```

We now have 749 files. With the following command, we save the filename of every files that does not contain the string Exception to *weka.classes*:

```
$ grep -L 'Exception' * | tee $WEKAPATH/weka.classes
```

This still comes down to 332 classes! Here are a few classes that might be of interest:

- attributeSelection.PrincipalComponents

- classifiers.bayes.NaiveBayes

- classifiers.evaluation.ConfusionMatrix

- `classifiers.functions.SimpleLinearRegression`
- `classifiers.meta.AdaBoostM1`
- `classifiers.trees.RandomForest`
- `clusterers.EM`
- `filters.unsupervised.attribute.Normalize`

As you can see, Weka offers a whole range of classes and functionality.

Adding tab completion

At this moment, you still need to type in the entire class name yourself. You can add so-called tab completion by adding the following snippet to your ~/.bashrc file after you export WEKAPATH:

```
_completeweka() {
  local curw=${COMP_WORDS[COMP_CWORD]}
  local wordlist=$(cat $WEKAPATH/weka.classes)
  COMPREPLY=($(compgen -W '${wordlist[@]}' -- "$curw"))
  return 0
}
complete -o nospace -F _completeweka weka
```

This function makes use of the *weka.classes* file we generated earlier. If you now type `weka clu` on the command line and press **<Tab>** three times, you're presented with a list of all classes that have to do with clustering:

```
$ weka clusterers.
clusterers.CheckClusterer
clusterers.CLOPE
clusterers.ClusterEvaluation
clusterers.Cobweb
clusterers.DBSCAN
clusterers.EM
clusterers.FarthestFirst
clusterers.FilteredClusterer
clusterers.forOPTICSAndDBScan.OPTICS_GUI.OPTICS_Visualizer
clusterers.HierarchicalClusterer
clusterers.MakeDensityBasedClusterer
clusterers.OPTICS
clusterers.sIB
clusterers.SimpleKMeans
clusterers.XMeans
```

Creating a command-line tool `weka`, determining the usable classes, and adding tab completion makes sure that Weka is a little bit easier to use at the command line.

Converting Between CSV and ARFF

Weka uses ARFF as a file format. This is basically CSV with additional information about the columns. We'll use two convenient command-line tools to convert between CSV and ARFF, namely csv2arff (see Example 9-1) and arff2csv (see Example 9-2).

Example 9-1. Convert CSV to ARFF (csv2arff)

```
#!/usr/bin/env bash
weka core.converters.CSVLoader /dev/stdin
```

Example 9-2. Convert ARFF to CSV (arff2csv)

```
#!/usr/bin/env bash
weka core.converters.CSVSaver -i /dev/stdin
```

Comparing Three Clustering Algorithms

In order to cluster data using Weka, we need yet another custom command-line tool to help us with this. The AddCluster class is needed to assign data points to the learned clusters. Unfortunately, this class does not accept data from standard input, not even when we specify -i /dev/stdin, because it expects a file with the *.arff* extension. We consider this to be bad design. The source code of weka-cluster is:

```
#!/usr/bin/env bash
ALGO="$@"
IN=$(mktemp --tmpdir weka-cluster-XXXXXXXX).arff

finish () {
        rm -f $IN
}
trap finish EXIT

csv2arff > $IN
weka filters.unsupervised.attribute.AddCluster -W "weka.${ALGO}" -i $IN \
-o /dev/stdout | arff2csv
```

Now we can apply the EM clustering algorithm and save the assignment as follows:

```
$ cd data
$ < wine-both-scaled.csv csvcut -C quality,type |          ❶
> weka-cluster clusterers.EM -N 5 |                         ❷
> csvcut -c cluster > data/wine-both-cluster-em.csv         ❸
```

❶ Use the scaled data set, and don't use the features quality and type for the clustering

❷ Apply the algorithm using weka-cluster

❸ Only save the cluster assignment

We'll run the same command again for the `SimpleKMeans` and `Cobweb` clustering algorithms. We now have three files with cluster assignments. Let's create a t-SNE mapping in order to visualize the cluster assignments:

```
$ < wine-both-scaled.csv csvcut -C quality,type | body tapkee --method t-sne |
> header -r x,y > wine-both-xy.csv
```

Next, the cluster assignments are combined with the t-SNE mapping using `paste` and a scatter plot is created using `Rio-scatter` (see Figures 9-5, 9-6, and 9-7):

```
$ parallel -j1 "paste -d, wine-both-xy.csv wine-both-cluster-{}.csv | "\
> "Rio-scatter x y cluster | display" ::: em simplekmeans cobweb
```

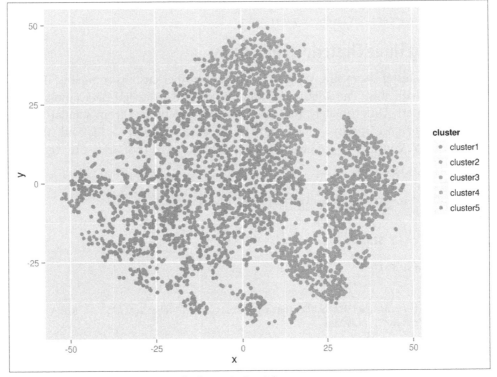

Figure 9-5. Clustering wines with the EM algorithm

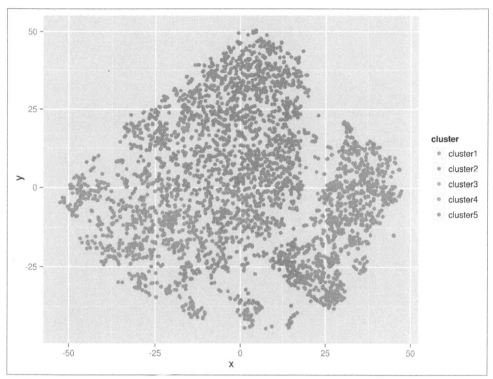

Figure 9-6. Clustering wines with the SimpleKMeans algorithm

Admittedly, we have gone through a lot of trouble taming Weka. The exercise was worth it, because some day you may run into a command-line tool that works differently from what you expect. Now you know that there are always ways to work around such command-line tools.

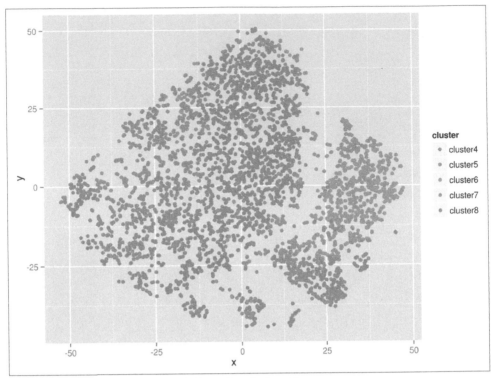

Figure 9-7. Clustering wines with the Cobweb algorithm

Regression with SciKit-Learn Laboratory

In this section, we'll be predicting the quality of the white wine, based on their physicochemical properties. Because the quality is a number between 0 and 10, we can consider predicting the quality as a regression task. Generally speaking, using training data points, we train three regression models using three different algorithms.

We'll be using the SciKit-Learn Laboratory (or SKLL) package for this. If you're not using the Data Science Toolbox, you can install SKLL using `pip`:

```
$ pip install skll
```

If you're running Python 2.7, you also need to install the following packages:

```
$ pip install configparser futures logutils
```

Preparing the Data

SKLL expects that the training and testing data have the same filenames, located in separate directories. However, in this example, we're going to use cross-validation, meaning that we only need to specify a training data set. Cross-validation is a technique that splits up the whole data set into a certain number of subsets. These subsets are called folds. (Usually, five or ten folds are used.)

We need to add an identifier to each row so that we can easily identify the data points later (the predictions are not in the same order as the original data set):

```
$ mkdir train
$ wine-white-clean.csv nl -s, -w1 -v0 | sed '1s/0,/id,/' > train/features.csv
```

Running the Experiment

Create a configuration file called *predict-quality.cfg*:

```
[General]
experiment_name = Wine
task = cross_validate

[Input]
train_location = train
featuresets = [["features.csv"]]
learners = ["LinearRegression","GradientBoostingRegressor","RandomForestRegres
sor"]
label_col = quality

[Tuning]
grid_search = false
feature_scaling = both
objective = r2

[Output]
log = output
results = output
predictions = output
```

We run the experiment using the run_experiment command-line tool (Educational Testing Service, 2014):

```
$ run_experiment -l predict-quality.cfg
```

The -l option specifies to run in local mode. SKLL also offers the possibility to run experiments on clusters. The time it takes to run the experiment depends on the complexity of the chosen algorithms.

Parsing the Results

Once all algorithms are done, the results can now be found in the directory *output*:

```
$ cd output
$ ls -1
Wine_features.csv_GradientBoostingRegressor.log
Wine_features.csv_GradientBoostingRegressor.predictions
Wine_features.csv_GradientBoostingRegressor.results
```

```
Wine_features.csv_GradientBoostingRegressor.results.json
Wine_features.csv_LinearRegression.log
Wine_features.csv_LinearRegression.predictions
Wine_features.csv_LinearRegression.results
Wine_features.csv_LinearRegression.results.json
Wine_features.csv_RandomForestRegressor.log
Wine_features.csv_RandomForestRegressor.predictions
Wine_features.csv_RandomForestRegressor.results
Wine_features.csv_RandomForestRegressor.results.json
Wine_summary.tsv
```

SKLL generates four files for each learner: one log, two with results, and one with predictions. Moreover, SKLL generates a summary file, which contains a lot of information about each individual fold (too much to show here). We can extract the relevant metrics using the following SQL query:

```
$ < Wine_summary.tsv csvsql --query "SELECT learner_name, pearson FROM stdin "\
> "WHERE fold = 'average' ORDER BY pearson DESC" | csvlook
|-----------------------------+----------------|
| learner_name                | pearson        |
|-----------------------------+----------------|
| RandomForestRegressor       | 0.741860521533 |
| GradientBoostingRegressor   | 0.661957860603 |
| LinearRegression            | 0.524144785555 |
|-----------------------------+----------------|
```

The relevant column here is `pearson`, which indicates the Pearson's ranking correlation. This is a value between −1 and 1 that indicates the correlation between the true ranking (of quality scores) and the predicted ranking. Let's paste all the predictions back to the data set:

```
$ parallel "csvjoin -c id train/features.csv <(< output/Wine_features.csv_{}"\
> ".predictions | tr '\t' ',') | csvcut -c id,quality,prediction > {}" ::: \
> RandomForestRegressor GradientBoostingRegressor LinearRegression
$ csvstack *Regres* -n learner --filenames > predictions.csv
```

And create a plot using `Rio` (see Figure 9-8):

```
$ < predictions.csv Rio -ge 'g+geom_point(aes(quality, round(prediction), '\
> 'color=learner), position="jitter", alpha=0.1) + facet_wrap(~ learner) + '\
> 'theme(aspect.ratio=1) + xlim(3,9) + ylim(3,9) + guides(colour=FALSE) + '\
> 'geom_smooth(aes(quality, prediction), method="lm", color="black") + '\
> 'ylab("prediction")' | display
```

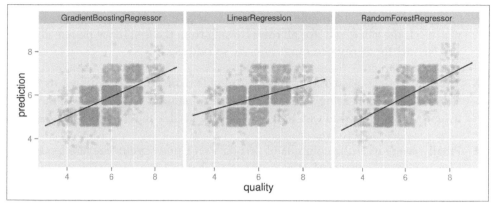

Figure 9-8. Comparing the output of three regression algorithms

Classification with BigML

In this fourth and last modeling section, we're going to classify wines as either red or white. For this we'll be using a solution called BigML, which provides a prediction API. This means that the actual modeling and predicting takes place in the cloud, which is useful if you need a bit more power than your own computer can offer.

Although prediction APIs are relatively young, they are becoming more prevalent, which is why we've included one in this chapter. Other prediction APIs include the Google Prediction API (*https://developers.google.com/prediction*) and PredictionIO (*http://prediction.io*). One advantage of BigML is that it offers a convenient command-line tool called bigmler (BigML, 2014) that interfaces with the API. We can use this command-line tool like any other presented in this book, except in this case behind the scenes, our data set is sent to BigML's servers, which perform the classification and send back the results.

Creating Balanced Train and Test Data Sets

First, we create a balanced data set to ensure that both classes are represented equally. For this, we use csvstack (Groskopf, 2014), shuf (Eggert, 2012), head, and csvcut:

```
$ csvstack -n type -g red,white wine-red-clean.csv \          ❶
> <(< wine-white-clean.csv body shuf | head -n 1600) |        ❷
> csvcut -c fixed_acidity,volatile_acidity,citric_acid,\       ❸
> residual_sugar,chlorides,free_sulfur_dioxide,total_sulfur_dioxide,\
> density,ph,sulphates,alcohol,type > wine-balanced.csv
```

This long command breaks down as follows:

❶ csvstack is used to combine multiple data sets. It creates a new column type, which has the value "red" for all rows coming from the first file *wine-red-clean.csv* and "white" for all rows coming from the second file.

❷ The second file is passed to csvstack using file redirection. This allows us to create a temporary file using shuf, which creates a random permutation of the *wine-white-clean.csv* and head which only selects the header and the first 1559 rows.

❸ Finally, we reorder the columns of this data set using csvcut because by default, bigmler assumes that the last column is the label.

Let's verify that *wine-balanced.csv* is actually balanced by counting the number of instances per class using parallel and grep:

```
$ parallel --tag grep -c {} wine-balanced.csv ::: red white
red        1599
white      1599
```

As you can see, the data set *wine-balanced.csv* contains both 1,599 red and 1,599 white wines. Next we split the data set into train and test data sets using split (Granlund & Stallman, 2012):

```
$ < wine-balanced.csv header > wine-header.csv                    ❶
$ tail -n +2 wine-balanced.csv | shuf | split -d -n r/2          ❷
$ parallel --xapply "cat wine-header.csv x0{1} > wine-{2}.csv" \  ❸
> ::: 0 1 ::: train test
```

This is another long command that deserves to be broken down:

❶ Get the header using header and save it to a temporary file named *wine-header.csv*.

❷ Mix up the red and white wines using tail and shuf and split it into two files named *x00* and *x01* using a round-robin distribution.

❸ Use cat to combine the header saved in *wine-header.csv* and the rows stored in *x00* to save it as *wine-train.csv*; similarly for *x01* and *wine-test.csv*. The --xapply option tells parallel to loop over the two input sources in tandem.

Let's check again the number of instances per class in both *wine-train.csv* and *wine-test.csv*:

```
$ parallel --tag grep -c {2} wine-{1}.csv ::: train test ::: red white
train red       821
train white     778
test white      821
test red        778
```

That looks like our data sets are well balanced. We're now ready to call the prediction API using `bigmler`.

Calling the API

 You can obtain a BigML username and API key at the BigML developer page (*https://bigml.com/developers*). Be sure to set the variables `BIGML_USERNAME` and `BIGML_API_KEY` in *~/.bashrc* with the appropriate values.

The API call is quite straightforward, and the meaning of each option is obvious from its name:

```
$ bigmler --train data/wine-train.csv \
> --test data/wine-test-blind.csv \
> --prediction-info full \
> --prediction-header \
> --output-dir output \
> --tag wine \
> --remote
```

The file *wine-test-blind.csv* is just *wine-test.csv* with the `type` column (the label) removed. After this call is finished, the results can be found in the *output* directory:

```
$ tree output
output
├── batch_prediction
├── bigmler_sessions
├── dataset
├── dataset_test
├── models
├── predictions.csv
├── source
└── source_test

0 directories, 8 files
```

Inspecting the Results

The file which is of most interest is *output/predictions.csv*:

```
$ csvcut output/predictions.csv -c type | head
type
white
white
red
red
white
red
```

```
red
white
red
```

We can compare these predicted labels with the labels in our test data set. Let's count the number of misclassifications:

```
$ paste -d, <(csvcut -c type data/wine-test.csv) \        ❶
> <(csvcut -c type output/predictions.csv) |
> awk -F, '{ if ($1 != $2) {sum+=1 } } END { print sum }'  ❷
766
```

❶ Combine the type columns of both *data/wine-test.csv* and *output/predictions.csv*.

❷ Keep count of when the two columns differ in value using awk.

As you can see, BigML's API misclassified 766 wines out of 1,599. This isn't a good result, but note that we just blindly applied an algorithm to a data set, which we normally wouldn't do. We can most probably achieve much better results if we would spend more time on tuning the features.

Conclusion

BigML's prediction API has proven to be very easy to use. As with many of the command-line tools discussed in this book, we've barely scratched the surface with BigML. You should also be aware of these additional features:

- BigML's command-line tool bigmler also allows for local computations, which is useful for debugging
- Results can also be inspected using BigML's web interface
- BigML can also perform regression tasks

For a complete overview of BigML's features, check out the developer page (*https:// bigml.com/developers*).

Although we've only been able to experiment with one prediction API, we believe that prediction APIs in general are worthwhile to consider for doing data science.

Further Reading

- Conway, D., & White, J. M. (2012). *Machine Learning for Hackers*. O'Reilly Media.
- Lisitsyn, S., Widmer, C., & Garcia, F. J. I. (2013). Tapkee: An Efficient Dimension Reduction Library. *Journal of Machine Learning Research*, 14, 2355–2359.

- Cortez, P., Cerdeira, A., Almeida, F., Matos, T., & Reis, J. (2009). Modeling Wine Preferences by Data Mining from Physicochemical Properties. *Decision Support Systems, 47*(4), 547–553.

- Hall, M., Frank, E., Holmes, G., Pfahringer, B., Reutemann, P., & Witten, I. H. (2009). The WEKA Data Mining Software: An Update. *SIGKDD Explorations, 11*(1).

- Pearson, K. (1901). On lines and planes of closest fit to systems of points in space. *Philosophical Magazine, 2*(11), 559–572.

- Van der Maaten, L., & Hinton, G. E. (2008). Visualizing Data using t-SNE. *Journal of Machine Learning Research, 9*, 2579–2605.

Conclusion

In this final chapter, the book comes to a close. We'll first recap what we have discussed in the previous nine chapters, and will then offer you three pieces of advice and provide some resources to further explore the related topics we touched upon. Finally, in case you have any questions, comments, or new command-line tools to share, we provide a few ways to get in touch.

Let's Recap

This book explored the power of employing the command line to perform data science tasks. It is an interesting observation that the challenges posed by this relatively young field can be tackled by such a time-tested technology. It is our hope that you now see what the command line is capable of. The many command-line tools offer all sorts of possibilities that are well suited to the variety of tasks encompassing data science.

There are many definitions for data science available. In Chapter 1, we introduced the OSEMN model as defined by Mason and Wiggens, because it is a very practical one that translates to very specific tasks. The acronym OSEMN stands for obtaining, scrubbing, exploring, modeling, and interpreting data. Chapter 1 also explained why the command line is very suitable for doing these data science tasks.

In Chapter 2, we explained how you can set up your own Data Science Toolbox and install the bundle that is associated with this book. Chapter 2 also provided an introduction to the essential tools and concepts of the command line.

The OSEMN model chapters—Chapters 3 (obtaining), 5 (scrubbing), 7 (exploring), and 9 (modeling)—focused on performing those practical tasks using the command line. We haven't deveoted a chapter to the fifth step, interpreting data, because, quite frankly, the computer, let alone the command line, is of very little use here. We have, however, provided some pointers for further reading on this topic.

In the three intermezzo chapters, we looked at some broader topics of doing data science at the command line, topics which are not really specific to one particular step. In Chapter 4, we explained how you can turn one-liners and existing code into reusable command-line tools. In Chapter 6, we described how you can manage your data workflow using a command-line tool called Drake. In Chapter 8, we demonstrated how ordinary command-line tools and pipelines can be run in parallel using GNU Parallel. These topics can be applied at any point in your data workflow.

It is impossible to demonstrate all command-line tools that are available and relevant for doing data science. New command-line tools are created on a daily basis. As you may have come to understand by now, this book is more about the idea of using the command line, rather than giving you an exhaustive list of tools.

Three Pieces of Advice

You probably spent quite some time reading these chapters and perhaps also following along with the code examples. In the hope that it maximizes the return on this investment and increases the probability that you'll continue to incorporate the command line into your data science workflow, we would like to offer you three pieces of advice: (1) be patient, (2) be creative, and (3) be practical. In the next three subsections we elaborate on each piece of advice.

Be Patient

The first piece of advice that we can give is to be patient. Working with data on the command line is different from using a programming language, and therefore it requires a different mindset.

Moreover, the command-line tools themselves are not without their quirks and inconsistencies. This is partly because they have been developed by many different people, over the course of multiple decades. If you ever find yourself at a loss regarding their mind-dazzling options, don't forget to use `--help`, man, or your favorite search engine to learn more.

Still, especially in the beginning, it can be a frustrating experience. Trust us, you will become more proficient as you practice using the command line and its tools. The command line has been around for many decades, and will be around for many more to come. It is a worthwhile investment.

Be Creative

The second, related piece of advice is to be creative. The command line is very flexible. By combining the command-line tools, you can accomplish more than you might think.

We encourage you to not immediately fall back onto your programming language. And when you do have to use a programming language, think about whether the code can be generalized or reused in some way. If so, consider creating your own command-line tool with that code using the steps we discussed in Chapter 4. If you believe your command-line tool may be beneficial for others, you could even go one step further by making it open source.

Be Practical

The third piece of advice is to be practical. Being practical is related to being creative, but deserves a separate explanation. In the previous subsection, we mentioned that you should not immediately fall back to a programming language. Of course, the command line has its limits. Throughout the book, we have emphasized that the command line should be regarded as a companion approach to doing data science.

We've discussed four steps for doing data science at the command line. In practice, the applicability of the command line is higher for step 1 than it is for step 4. You should use whatever approach works best for the task at hand. And it's perfectly fine to mix and match approaches at any point in your workflow. The command line is wonderful at being integrated with other approaches, programming languages, and statistical environments. There's a certain trade-off with each approach, and part of becoming proficient at the command line is to learn when to use which.

In conclusion, when you're patient, creative, and practical, the command line will make you a more efficient and productive data scientist.

Where to Go from Here?

As this book is on the intersection of the command line and data science, many related topics have only been touched upon. Now, it's up to you to further explore these topics. The following subsections provide a list of topics and suggested resources to consult.

APIs

- Russell, M. (2013). Mining the Social Web (2nd Ed.). O'Reilly Media.
- Warden, P. (2011). Data Source Handbook. O'Reilly Media.

Shell Programming

- Winterbottom, D. (2014). commandlinefu.com. Retrieved from *http://www.commandlinefu.com*.
- Peek, J., Powers, S., O'Reilly, T., & Loukides, M. (2002). Unix Power Tools (3rd Ed.). O'Reilly Media.
- Goyvaerts, J., & Levithan, S. (2012). *Regular Expressions Cookbook* (2nd Ed.). O'Reilly Media.
- Cooper, M. (2014). "Advanced Bash-Scripting Guide." Retrieved May 10, 2014, from *http://www.tldp.org/LDP/abs/html*.
- Robbins, A., & Beebe, N. H. F. (2005). Classic Shell Scripting. O'Reilly Media.

Python, R, and SQL

- Wickham, H. (2009). *ggplot2: Elegant Graphics for Data Analysis*. Springer.
- McKinney, W. (2012). Python for Data Analysis. O'Reilly Media.
- Rossant, C. (2013). *Learning IPython for Interactive Computing and Data Visualization*. Packt Publishing.

Interpreting Data

- Shron, M. (2014). Thinking with Data. O'Reilly Media.
- Patil, D. J. (2012). "Data Jujitsu". O'Reilly Media.

Getting in Touch

This book would not have been possible without the many people who created the command line and the numerous command-line tools. It's safe to say that the current ecosystem of command-line tools for data science is a community effort. We have only been able to give you a glimpse of the many command-line tools available. New ones are created everyday, and perhaps some day you will create one yourself. In that case, we would love to hear from you. We'd also appreciate it if you would drop us a line whenever you have a question, comment, or suggestion. There are a couple of ways to get in touch:

- Email: *jeroen@jeroenjanssens.com*
- Twitter: *@jeroenhjanssens*
- Book website: *http://datascienceatthecommandline.com/*
- GitHub: *https://github.com/jeroenjanssens/data-science-at-the-command-line*

List of Command-Line Tools

This is an overview of all the command-line tools discussed in this book. This includes binary executables, interpreted scripts, and Bash builtins and keywords. For each command-line tool, the following information, when available and appropriate, is provided:

- The actual command to type at the commandline
- A description
- The name of the package it belongs to
- The version used in the book
- The year that version was released
- The primary author(s)
- A website to find more information
- How to install it
- How to obtain help
- An example usage

All command-line tools listed here are included in the Data Science Toolbox for *Data Science at the Command Line*. See Chapter 2 for instructions on how to set it up. The install commands assume that you're running Ubuntu 14.04. Please note that citing open source software is not trivial, and that some information may be missing or incorrect.

alias

Define or display aliases. Alias is a Bash builtin.

```
$ help alias
$ alias ll='ls -alF'
```

awk

Pattern scanning and text processing language. Mawk (version 1.3.3) by Mike
Brennan (1994). *http://invisible-island.net/mawk*.

```
$ sudo apt-get install mawk
$ man awk
$ seq 5 | awk '{sum+=$1} END {print sum}'
15
```

aws

Manage AWS Services such as EC2 and S3 from the command line. AWS Command
Line Interface (version 1.3.24) by Amazon Web Services (2014). *http://
aws.amazon.com/cli*.

```
$ sudo pip install awscli
$ aws help
$ aws ec2 describe-regions | head -n 5
{
    "Regions": [
        {
            "Endpoint": "ec2.eu-west-1.amazonaws.com",
            "RegionName": "eu-west-1"
```

bash

GNU Bourne-Again SHell. Bash (version 4.3) by Brian Fox and Chet Ramey (2010).
http://www.gnu.org/software/bash.

```
$ sudo apt-get install bash
$ man bash
```

bc

Evaluate equation from standard input. Bc (version 1.06.95) by Philip A. Nelson
(2006). *http://www.gnu.org/software/bc*.

```
$ sudo apt-get install bc
$ man bc
$ echo 'e(1)' | bc -l
2.71828182845904523536
```

bigmler

Access BigML's prediction API. BigMLer (version 1.12.2) by BigML (2014). *http://bigmler.readthedocs.org.*

```
$ sudo pip install bigmler
$ bigmler --help
```

body

Apply an expression to all but the first line. Useful if you want to apply classic command-line tools to CSV files with a header. Body by Jeroen H.M. Janssens (2014). *https://github.com/jeroenjanssens/data-science-at-the-command-line.*

```
$ git clone https://github.com/jeroenjanssens/data-science-at-the-command-
line.git
$ echo -e "value\n7\n2\n5\n3" | body sort -n
value
2
3
5
7
```

cat

Concatenate files and standard input, and print on standard output. Cat (version 8.21) by Torbjorn Granlund and Richard M. Stallman (2012). *http://www.gnu.org/software/coreutils.*

```
$ sudo apt-get install coreutils
$ man cat
$ cat results-01 results-02 results-03 > results-all
```

cd

Change the shell working directory. Cd is a Bash builtin.

```
$ help cd
$ cd ~; pwd; cd ..; pwd
/home/vagrant
/home
```

chmod

Change file mode bits. We use it to make our command-line tools executable. Chmod (version 8.21) by David MacKenzie and Jim Meyering (2012). *http://www.gnu.org/software/coreutils.*

```
$ sudo apt-get install coreutils
$ man chmod
$ chmod u+x experiment.sh
```

cols

Apply a command to a subset of the columns and merge the result back with the remaining columns. Cols by Jeroen H.M. Janssens (2014). *https://github.com/jeroen janssens/data-science-at-the-command-line.*

```
$ git clone https://github.com/jeroenjanssens/data-science-at-the-command-
line.git
$ < iris.csv cols -C species body tapkee --method pca | header -r x,y,species
```

cowsay

Generate an ASCII picture of a cow with a message. Useful for when building up a particular pipeline is starting to frustrate you a bit too much. Cowsay (version 3.03+dfsg1) by Tony Monroe (1999).

```
$ sudo apt-get install cowsay
$ man cowsay
$ echo 'The command line is awesome!' | cowsay
 _____
< The command line is awesome! >
 -----------------------------
        \   ^__^
         \  (oo)_____
            (__)\       )\/\
                ||----w |
                ||     ||
```

cp

Copy files and directories. Cp (version 8.21) by Torbjorn Granlund, David MacKenzie, and Jim Meyering (2012). *http://www.gnu.org/software/coreutils.*

```
$ sudo apt-get install coreutils
$ man cp
```

csvcut

Extract columns from CSV data. Like cut command-line tool, but for tabular data. Csvkit (version 0.8.0) by Christopher Groskopf (2014). *http://csvkit.readthedocs.org.*

```
$ sudo pip install csvkit
$ csvcut --help
```

csvgrep

Filter tabular data to only those rows where certain columns contain a given value or match a regular expression. Csvkit (version 0.8.0) by Christopher Groskopf (2014). *http://csvkit.readthedocs.org.*

```
$ sudo pip install csvkit
$ csvgrep --help
```

csvjoin

Merge two or more CSV tables together using a method analogous to a SQL JOIN operation. Csvkit (version 0.8.0) by Christopher Groskopf (2014). *http://csvkit.read thedocs.org.*

```
$ sudo pip install csvkit
$ csvjoin --help
```

csvlook

Renders a CSV file to the command line in a readable, fixed-width format. Csvkit (version 0.8.0) by Christopher Groskopf (2014). *http://csvkit.readthedocs.org.*

```
$ sudo pip install csvkit
$ csvlook --help
$ echo -e "a,b\n1,2\n3,4" | csvlook
|----+----|
|  a | b  |
|----+----|
|  1 | 2  |
|  3 | 4  |
|----+----|
```

csvsort

Sort CSV files. Like the `sort` command-line tool, but for tabular data. Csvkit (version 0.8.0) by Christopher Groskopf (2014). *http://csvkit.readthedocs.org.*

```
$ sudo pip install csvkit
$ csvsort --help
```

csvsql

Execute SQL queries directly on CSV data or insert CSV into a database. Csvkit (version 0.8.0) by Christopher Groskopf (2014). *http://csvkit.readthedocs.org.*

```
$ sudo pip install csvkit
$ csvsql --help
```

csvstack

Stack up the rows from multiple CSV files, optionally adding a grouping value to each row. Csvkit (version 0.8.0) by Christopher Groskopf (2014). *http://csvkit.readthe docs.org.*

```
$ sudo pip install csvkit
$ csvstack --help
```

csvstat

Print descriptive statistics for all columns in a CSV file. Csvkit (version 0.8.0) by Christopher Groskopf (2014). *http://csvkit.readthedocs.org.*

```
$ sudo pip install csvkit
$ csvstat --help
```

curl

Download data from a URL. cURL (version 7.35.0) by Daniel Stenberg (2012). *http:// curl.haxx.se.*

```
$ sudo apt-get install curl
$ man curl
```

curlicue

Perform OAuth dance for `curl`. Curlicue by Decklin Foster (2014). *https:// github.com/decklin/curlicue.*

```
$ git clone https://github.com/decklin/curlicue.git
```

cut

Remove sections from each line of files. Cut (version 8.21) by David M. Ihnat, David MacKenzie, and Jim Meyering (2012). *http://www.gnu.org/software/coreutils.*

```
$ sudo apt-get install coreutils
$ man cut
```

display

Display an image or image sequence on any X server. Can read image data from standard input. Display (version 8:6.7.7.10) by ImageMagick Studio LLC (2009). *http:// www.imagemagick.org.*

```
$ sudo apt-get install imagemagick
$ man display
```

drake

Manage a data workflow. Drake (version 0.1.6) by Factual (2014). *https://github.com/Factual/drake*.

```
$ # Please see Chapter 6 for installation instructions.
$ drake --help
```

dseq

Generate sequence of dates relative to today. Dseq by Jeroen H.M. Janssens (2014). *https://github.com/jeroenjanssens/data-science-at-the-command-line*.

```
$ git clone https://github.com/jeroenjanssens/data-science-at-the-command-
line.git
$ dseq -2 0 # day before yesterday till today
2014-07-15
2014-07-16
2014-07-17
```

echo

Display a line of text. Echo (version 8.21) by Brian Fox and Chet Ramey (2012). *http://www.gnu.org/software/coreutils*.

```
$ sudo apt-get install coreutils
$ man echo
```

env

Run a program in a modified environment. It's often used to specify which interpreter should run our script. Env (version 8.21) by Richard Mlynarik and David MacKenzie (2012). *http://www.gnu.org/software/coreutils*.

```
$ sudo apt-get install coreutils
$ man env
$ #!/usr/bin/env python
```

export

Set export attribute for shell variables. Useful for making shell variables available to other command-line tools. Export is a Bash builtin.

```
$ help export
$ export WEKAPATH=$HOME/bin
```

feedgnuplot

Generate a script for `gnuplot` while passing data to standard input. Feedgnuplot (version 1.32) by Dima Kogan (2014). *http://search.cpan.org/perldoc?feedgnuplot*.

```
$ sudo apt-get install feedgnuplot
$ man feedgnuplot
```

fieldsplit

Splits a file into multiple files according to a particular field value. Fieldsplit (version 2010-01) by Jeremy Hinds, Jason Gessner, Jim Renwick, Norman Gocke, Rodofo Granata, and Tobias Wolff (2010). *http://code.google.com/p/crush-tools*.

```
$ # See website for installation instructions
$ fieldsplit --help
```

find

Search for files in a directory hierarchy. Find (version 4.4.2) by James Youngman (2008). *http://www.gnu.org/software/findutils*.

```
$ sudo apt-get install findutils
$ man find
```

for

Execute commands for each member in a list. In Chapter 8, we discuss the advantages of using `parallel` instead of `for`. For is a Bash keyword.

```
$ help for
$ for i in {A..C} "It's easy as" {1..3}; do echo $i; done
A
B
C
It's easy as
1
2
3
```

git

Manage repositories for Git, which is a distributed version control system. Git (version 1:1.9.1) by Linus Torvalds and Junio C. Hamano (2014). *http://git-scm.com*.

```
$ sudo apt-get install git
$ man git
```

grep

Print lines matching a pattern. Grep (version 2.16) by Jim Meyering (2012). *http:// www.gnu.org/software/grep.*

```
$ sudo apt-get install grep
$ man grep
```

head

Output the first part of files. Head (version 8.21) by David MacKenzie and Jim Meyering (2012). *http://www.gnu.org/software/coreutils.*

```
$ sudo apt-get install coreutils
$ man head
$ seq 5 | head -n 3
1
2
3
```

header

Add, replace, and delete header lines. Header by Jeroen H.M. Janssens (2014). *https:// github.com/jeroenjanssens/data-science-at-the-command-line.*

```
$ git clone https://github.com/jeroenjanssens/data-science-at-the-command-
line.git
$ header -h
```

in2csv

Convert common, but less awesome, tabular data formats to CSV. Csvkit (version 0.8.0) by Christopher Groskopf (2014). *http://csvkit.readthedocs.org.*

```
$ sudo pip install csvkit
$ in2csv --help
```

jq

Process JSON. Jq (version jq-1.4) by Stephen Dolan (2014). *http://stedo lan.github.com/jq.*

```
$ # See website for installation instructions
$ # See website for documentation
```

json2csv

Convert JSON to CSV. Json2Csv (version 1.1) by Jehiah Czebotar (2014). *https://github.com/jehiah/json2csv.*

```
$ go get github.com/jehiah/json2csv
$ json2csv --help
```

less

Paginate large files. Less (version 458) by Mark Nudelman (2013). *http://www.greenwoodsoftware.com/less.*

```
$ sudo apt-get install less
$ man less
$ csvlook iris.csv | less
```

ls

List directory contents. Ls (version 8.21) by Richard M. Stallman and David MacKenzie (2012). *http://www.gnu.org/software/coreutils.*

```
$ sudo apt-get install coreutils
$ man ls
```

man

Read reference manuals of command-line tools. Man (version 2.6.7.1) by John W. Eaton and Colin Watson (2014).

```
$ sudo apt-get install man
$ man man
$ man grep
```

mkdir

Make directories. Mkdir (version 8.21) by David MacKenzie (2012). *http://www.gnu.org/software/coreutils.*

```
$ sudo apt-get install coreutils
$ man mkdir
```

mv

Move or rename files and directories. Mv (version 8.21) by Mike Parker, David MacKenzie, and Jim Meyering (2012). *http://www.gnu.org/software/coreutils.*

```
$ sudo apt-get install coreutils
$ man mv
```

parallel

Build and execute shell command lines from standard input in parallel. GNU Parallel (version 20140622) by Ole Tange (2014). *http://www.gnu.org/software/parallel*.

```
$ # See website for installation instructions
$ man parallel
$ seq 3 | parallel echo Processing file {}.csv
Processing file 1.csv
Processing file 2.csv
Processing file 3.csv
```

paste

Merge lines of files. Paste (version 8.21) by David M. Ihnat and David MacKenzie (2012). *http://www.gnu.org/software/coreutils*.

```
$ sudo apt-get install coreutils
$ man paste
```

pbc

Run bc with `parallel`. First column of input CSV is mapped to {1}, second to {2}, and so forth. Pbc by Jeroen H.M. Janssens (2014). *https://github.com/jeroenjanssens/data-science-at-the-command-line*.

```
$ git clone https://github.com/jeroenjanssens/data-science-at-the-command-
line.git
$ seq 5 | pbc '{1}^2'
1
4
9
16
25
```

pip

Install and manage Python packages. Pip (version 1.5.4) by PyPA (2014). *https://pip.pypa.io*.

```
$ sudo apt-get install python-pip
$ man pip
```

pwd

Print name of current working directory. Pwd (version 8.21) is a Bash builtin by Jim Meyering (2012). *http://www.gnu.org/software/coreutils*.

```
$ man pwd
$ pwd
/home/vagrant
```

python

Execute Python, which is an interpreted, interactive, and object-oriented programming language. Python (version 2.7.5) by Python Software Foundation (2014). *http://www.python.org*.

```
$ sudo apt-get install python
$ man python
```

R

Analyze data and create visualizations with the R programming language. To install the latest version of R on Ubuntu, follow the instructions on *http://bit.ly/ubuntu_packages_for_R*. R (version 3.1.1) by R Foundation for Statistical Computing (2014). *http://www.r-project.org*.

```
$ sudo apt-get install r-base-dev
$ man R
```

Rio

Load CSV from standard input into R as a data.frame, execute given commands, and get the output as CSV or PNG. Rio by Jeroen H.M. Janssens (2014). *https://github.com/jeroenjanssens/data-science-at-the-command-line*.

```
$ git clone https://github.com/jeroenjanssens/data-science-at-the-command-
line.git
$ Rio -h
$ seq 10 | Rio -nf sum
55
```

Rio-scatter

Create a scatter plot from CSV using Rio. Rio-scatter by Jeroen H.M. Janssens (2014). *https://github.com/jeroenjanssens/data-science-at-the-command-line*.

```
$ git clone https://github.com/jeroenjanssens/data-science-at-the-command-
line.git
$ < iris.csv Rio-scatter sepal_length sepal_width species > iris.png
```

rm

Remove files or directories. Rm (version 8.21) by Paul Rubin, David MacKenzie, Richard M. Stallman, and Jim Meyering (2012). *http://www.gnu.org/software/coreutils*.

```
$ sudo apt-get install coreutils
$ man rm
```

run_experiment

Run machine learning experiments with the Python package scikit-learn. SciKit-Learn Laboratory (version 0.26.0) by Educational Testing Service (2014). *https://skll.readthedocs.org*.

```
$ sudo pip install skll
$ run_experiment --help
```

sample

Print lines from standard output with a given probability, for a given duration, and with a given delay between lines. Sample by Jeroen H.M. Janssens (2014). *https://github.com/jeroenjanssens/data-science-at-the-command-line*.

```
$ git clone https://github.com/jeroenjanssens/data-science-at-the-command-
line.git
$ sample --help
```

scp

Copy remote files securely. Scp (version 1:6.6p1) by Timo Rinne and Tatu Ylonen (2014). *http://www.openssh.com*.

```
$ sudo apt-get install openssh-client
$ man scp
```

scrape

Extract HTML elements using an XPath query or CSS3 selector. Scrape by Jeroen H.M. Janssens (2014). *https://github.com/jeroenjanssens/data-science-at-the-command-line*.

```
$ git clone https://github.com/jeroenjanssens/data-science-at-the-command-
line.git
$ curl -sL 'http://datasciencetoolbox.org' | scrape -e 'head > title'
<title>Data Science Toolbox</title>
```

sed

Filter and transform text. Sed (version 4.2.2) by Jay Fenlason, Tom Lord, Ken Pizzini, and Paolo Bonzini (2012). *http://www.gnu.org/software/sed.*

```
$ sudo apt-get install sed
$ man sed
```

seq

Print a sequence of numbers. Seq (version 8.21) by Ulrich Drepper (2012). *http://www.gnu.org/software/coreutils.*

```
$ sudo apt-get install coreutils
$ man seq
$ seq 5
1
2
3
4
5
```

shuf

Generate random permutations. Shuf (version 8.21) by Paul Eggert (2012). *http://www.gnu.org/software/coreutils.*

```
$ sudo apt-get install coreutils
$ man shuf
```

sort

Sort lines of text files. Sort (version 8.21) by Mike Haertel and Paul Eggert (2012). *http://www.gnu.org/software/coreutils.*

```
$ sudo apt-get install coreutils
$ man sort
```

split

Split a file into pieces. Split (version 8.21) by Torbjorn Granlund and Richard M. Stallman (2012). *http://www.gnu.org/software/coreutils.*

```
$ sudo apt-get install coreutils
$ man split
```

sql2csv

Executes arbitrary commands against an SQL database and outputs the results as a CSV. Csvkit (version 0.8.0) by Christopher Groskopf (2014). *http://csvkit.readthe docs.org.*

```
$ sudo pip install csvkit
$ sql2csv --help
```

ssh

Login to remote machines. OpenSSH client (version 1.8.9) by Tatu Ylonen, Aaron Campbell, Bob Beck, Markus Friedl, Niels Provos, Theo de Raadt, Dug Song, and Markus Friedl (2014). *http://www.openssh.com.*

```
$ sudo apt-get install ssh
$ man ssh
```

sudo

Execute a command as another user. Sudo (version 1.8.9p5) by Todd C. Miller (2013). *http://www.sudo.ws/sudo.*

```
$ sudo apt-get install sudo
$ man sudo
```

tail

Output the last part of files. Tail (version 8.21) by Paul Rubin, David MacKenzie, Ian Lance Taylor, and Jim Meyering (2012). *http://www.gnu.org/software/coreutils.*

```
$ sudo apt-get install coreutils
$ man tail
$ seq 5 | tail -n 3
3
4
5
```

tapkee

Reduce dimensionality of a data set using various algorithms. Tapkee by Sergey Lisit-syn and Fernando Iglesias (2014). *http://tapkee.lisitsyn.me.*

```
$ # See website for installation instructions
$ tapkee --help
$ < iris.csv cols -C species body tapkee --method pca | header -r x,y,species
```

tar

Create, list, and extract TAR archives. Tar (version 1.27.1) by Jeff Bailey, Paul Eggert, and Sergey Poznyakoff (2014). *http://www.gnu.org/software/tar.*

```
$ sudo apt-get install tar
$ man tar
```

tee

Read from standard input and write to standard output and files. Tee (version 8.21) by Mike Parker, Richard M. Stallman, and David MacKenzie (2012). *http://www.gnu.org/software/coreutils.*

```
$ sudo apt-get install coreutils
$ man tee
```

tr

Translate or delete characters. Tr (version 8.21) by Jim Meyering (2012). *http://www.gnu.org/software/coreutils.*

```
$ sudo apt-get install coreutils
$ man tr
```

tree

List contents of directories in a tree-like format. Tree (version 1.6.0) by Steve Baker (2014). *https://launchpad.net/ubuntu/+source/tree.*

```
$ sudo apt-get install tree
$ man tree
```

type

Display the type of a command-line tool. Type is a Bash builtin.

```
$ help type
$ type cd
cd is a shell builtin
```

uniq

Report or omit repeated lines. Uniq (version 8.21) by Richard M. Stallman and David MacKenzie (2012). *http://www.gnu.org/software/coreutils.*

```
$ sudo apt-get install coreutils
$ man uniq
```

unpack

Extract common file formats. Unpack by Patrick Brisbin (2013). *https://github.com/ jeroenjanssens/data-science-at-the-command-line.*

```
$ git clone https://github.com/jeroenjanssens/data-science-at-the-command-
line.git
$ unpack file.tgz
```

unrar

Extract files from RAR archives. Unrar (version 1:0.0.1+cvs20071127) by Ben Asselstine, Christian Scheurer, and Johannes Winkelmann (2014). *http://home.gna.org/ unrar.*

```
$ sudo apt-get install unrar-free
$ man unrar
```

unzip

List, test and extract compressed files in a ZIP archive. Unzip (version 6.0) by Samuel H. Smith (2009).

```
$ sudo apt-get install unzip
$ man unzip
```

wc

Print newline, word, and byte counts for each file. Wc (version 8.21) by Paul Rubin and David MacKenzie (2012). *http://www.gnu.org/software/coreutils.*

```
$ sudo apt-get install coreutils
$ man wc
$ echo 'hello world' | wc -c
12
```

weka

Weka is a collection of machine learning algorithms for data mining tasks by Mark Hall, Eibe Frank, Geoffrey Holmes, Bernhard Pfahringer, Peter Reutemann, and Ian H. Witten. This command-line tool allows you to run Weka from the command line. Weka command-line tool by Jeroen H.M. Janssens (2014). *https://github.com/jeroen janssens/data-science-at-the-command-line.*

```
$ git clone https://github.com/jeroenjanssens/data-science-at-the-command-
line.git
```

which

Locate a command-line tool. Does not work for Bash builtins. Which by unknown (2009).

```
$ man which
$ which man
/usr/bin/man
```

xml2json

Convert XML to JSON. Xml2Json (version 0.0.2) by Francois Parmentier (2014). *https://github.com/parmentf/xml2json*.

```
$ npm install xml2json-command
$ xml2json < input.xml > output.json
```

Bibliography

Amazon Web Services (2014). AWS Command Line Interface Documentation. Retrieved from *http://aws.amazon.com/documentation/cli/*.

Conway, D., & White, J. M. (2012). *Machine Learning for Hackers*. O'Reilly Media.

Cooper, M. (2014). Advanced Bash-Scripting Guide. Retrieved May 10, 2014, from *http://www.tldp.org/LDP/abs/html*.

Cortez, P., Cerdeira, A., Almeida, F., Matos, T., & Reis, J. (2009). Modeling Wine Preferences by Data Mining from Physicochemical Properties. *Decision Support Systems*, *47*(4), 547–553.

Docopt. (2014). Command-line Interface Description Language. Retrieved from *http://docopt.org*.

Dougherty, D., & Robbins, A. (1997). *sed & awk* (2nd Ed.). O'Reilly Media.

Goyvaerts, J., & Levithan, S. (2012). *Regular Expressions Cookbook* (2nd Ed.). O'Reilly Media.

Hall, M., Frank, E., Holmes, G., Pfahringer, B., Reutemann, P., & Witten, I. H. (2009). The WEKA Data Mining Software: An Update. *SIGKDD Explorations*, *11*(1).

HashiCorp. (2014). Vagrant. Retrieved May 10, 2014, from *http://vagrantup.com*.

Heddings, L. (2006). Keyboard Shortcuts for Bash. Retrieved May 10, 2014, from *http://www.howtogeek.com/howto/ubuntu/keyboard-shortcuts-for-bash-command-shell-for-ubuntu-debian-suse-redhat-linux-etc*.

Janert, P. K. (2009). *Gnuplot in Action*. Manning Publications.

Janssens, J. H. M. (2014). Data Science Toolbox. Retrieved May 10, 2014, from *http://datasciencetoolbox.org*.

Lisitsyn, S., Widmer, C., & Garcia, F. J. I. (2013). Tapkee: An Efficient Dimension Reduction Library. *Journal of Machine Learning Research, 14,* 2355–2359.

Mason, H., & Wiggins, C. H. (2010). A Taxonomy of Data Science. Retrieved May 10, 2014, from *http://www.dataists.com/2010/09/a-taxonomy-of-data-science.*

McKinney, W. (2012). *Python for Data Analysis.* O'Reilly Media.

Molinaro, A. (2005). *SQL Cookbook.* O'Reilly Media.

Oracle. (2014). VirtualBox. Retrieved May 10, 2014, from *http://virtualbox.org.*

Patil, D. (2012). Data Jujitsu. O'Reilly Media.

Pearson, K. (1901). On lines and planes of closest fit to systems of points in space. *Philosophical Magazine, 2*(11), 559–572.

Peek, J., Powers, S., O'Reilly, T., & Loukides, M. (2002). *Unix Power Tools* (3rd Ed.). O'Reilly Media.

Perkins, J. (2010). *Python Text Processing with NLTK 2.0 Cookbook.* Packt Publishing.

Raymond, E. S. (2014). Basics of the Unix Philosophy. Retrieved from *http://www.faqs.org/docs/artu/ch01s06.html.*

Robbins, A., & Beebe, N. H. F. (2005). *Classic Shell Scripting.* O'Reilly Media.

Rossant, C. (2013). *Learning IPython for Interactive Computing and Data Visualization.* Packt Publishing.

Russell, M. (2013). *Mining the Social Web* (2nd Ed.). O'Reilly Media.

O'Neil, C., & Schutt, R. (2013). *Doing Data Science.* O'Reilly Media.

Shron, M. (2014). *Thinking with Data.* O'Reilly Media.

Tange, O. (2011). GNU Parallel—The Command-Line Power Tool. *;Login: The USENIX Magazine, 36*(1), 42–47. Retrieved from *http://www.gnu.org/s/parallel.*

Tange, O. (2014). GNU Parallel Tutorial. Retrieved from *http://www.gnu.org/software/parallel/parallel_tutorial.html.*

Tukey, J. W. (1977). *Exploratory Data Analysis.* Pearson.

Van der Maaten, L., & Hinton, G. E. (2008). "Visualizing Data Using t-SNE." *Journal of Machine Learning Research, 9,* 2579–2605.

Warden, P. (2011). *Data Source Handbook.* O'Reilly Media.

Wickham, H. (2009). *ggplot2: Elegant Graphics for Data Analysis.* Springer.

Wiggins, C. (2014). Public Aliases. Retrieved May 10, 2014, from *https://github.com/chrishwiggins/mise/blob/master/sh/aliases-public.sh.*

Wikipedia. (2014). List of HTTP status codes. Retrieved May 10, 2014, from *http://en.wikipedia.org/wiki/List_of_HTTP_status_codes*.

Winterbottom, D. (2014). commandlinefu.com. Retrieved from *http://www.commandlinefu.com*.

Wirzenius, L. (2013). "Writing Manual Pages." Retrieved from *http://liw.fi/manpages/*.

Index

python, 176

R

R, 49-52, 99-102, 176
regression, 150-152
regular expression, 58-62
remote machine, 125
    distributing data to, 128-129
    processing files on, 129-132
    running commands on, 127-128
replacing/deleting values, 62
resources for further exploration, 161
Rio, 11, 99-102, 105, 114, 141, 152, 176
Rio-scatter, 176
rm, 25, 177
run_experiment, 151, 177

S

sample, 59, 177
scalability, 8
scatter plot, 112-112
SciKit-Learn Laboratory (SKLL), 150-152
scp, 31, 177
scrape, 69, 177
scrubbing data, 55-80
    bodies, headers, and columns, 62-66
    combining multiple CSV files, 77-80
    CSV operations, 72-80
    extracting and reordering columns, 72-73
    extracting values, 60-61
    filtering lines, 57-60, 73-75
    in CSV, 62-67
    merging columns, 75-77
    operations for plain text, 56-62
    overview, 3
    replacing and deleting values, 62
    SQL queries, 67
sed, 55, 57, 60, 68, 78, 105, 178
seq, 18, 23, 178
serial processing, 116-119
server (see remote machine)
shebangs, 46
shell, 18
shell builtins, 20
shell functions, 21
shell scripts, 42-49
    access permissions, 45-46
    and workflow management, 81
    creating new file, 44

defining shebang, 46
extending PATH, 48-49
parameters, 47-48
porting to Python and R, 50-52
removing fixed input, 47
shuf, 153, 178
SimpleKMeans, 148, 149
sort, 178
split, 154, 178
SQL queries, 67
sql2csv, 35, 179
SSH, 125, 127
ssh, 179
streaming data, 52
subshells, 120
sudo, 179

T

t-SNE (t-Distributed Stochastic Neighbor
    Embedding), 140
tail, 57, 179
tapkee, 140, 179
tar, 31, 180
tee, 79, 180
terminal, 5, 18
text scrubbing, 56-62
tool, 4, 14, 18
    (see also command-line tools)
tr, 62, 137, 180
tree, 10, 180
type, 22, 27, 180

U

Ubuntu, 13
    (see also GNU/Linux)
uniq, 180
Unix
    philosophy, 23, 29, 41
    pipe, 23
unpack, 31, 181
unrar, 31, 181
unzip, 31, 181

V

Vagrant, 14
VirtualBox, 14
visualizing data, 91, 102-114
    bar plot, 108-110

About the Author

Jeroen Janssens is a senior data scientist at YPlan, tonight's going out app, where he's responsible for making event recommendations more personal. Jeroen holds an MSc in Artificial Intelligence from Maastricht University and a PhD in Machine Learning from Tilburg University. Jeroen enjoys biking the Brooklyn Bridge, building tools, and blogging at *http://jeroenjanssens.com*.

Colophon

The animal on the cover of *Data Science at the Command Line* is a wreathed hornbill (*Rhytidoceros undulatus*). Also known as the bar-pouched wreathed hornbill, the species is found in forests in mainland Southeast Asia and in northeastern India and Bhutan. Hornbills are named for the *casques* that form on the upper part of the birds' bills. No single obvious purpose exists for these hollow, keratinized structures, but they may serve as a means of recognition between members of the species, as an amplifier for the birds' calls, or—because males often exhibit larger casques than females of the species—for gender recognition. Wreathed hornbills can be distinguished from plain-pouched hornbills, to whom they are closely related and otherwise similar in appearance, by a dark bar on the lower part of the wreathed hornbills' throats.

Wreathed hornbills roost in flocks of up to 400 but mate in monogamous, lifelong partnerships. With help from the males, females seal themselves up in tree cavities behind dung and mud to lay eggs and brood. Through a slit large enough for his beak alone, the male feeds his mate and their young for up to four months. A diet of animal prey becomes predominantly fruit when females and their young leave the nest. Hornbill couples have been known to return to the same nest for as many as nine years.

Many of the animals on O'Reilly covers are endangered; all of them are important to the world. To learn more about how you can help, go to *animals.oreilly.com*.

The cover image is from Hungarian plates. The cover fonts are URW Typewriter and Guardian Sans. The text font is Adobe Minion Pro; the heading font is Adobe Myriad Condensed; and the code font is Dalton Maag's Ubuntu Mono.

Get even more for your money.

Join the O'Reilly Community, and register the O'Reilly books you own. It's free, and you'll get:

- $4.99 ebook upgrade offer
- 40% upgrade offer on O'Reilly print books
- Membership discounts on books and events
- Free lifetime updates to ebooks and videos
- Multiple ebook formats, DRM FREE
- Participation in the O'Reilly community
- Newsletters
- Account management
- 100% Satisfaction Guarantee

Signing up is easy:

1. Go to: oreilly.com/go/register
2. Create an O'Reilly login.
3. Provide your address.
4. Register your books.

Note: English-language books only

To order books online:
oreilly.com/store

For questions about products or an order:
orders@oreilly.com

To sign up to get topic-specific email announcements and/or news about upcoming books, conferences, special offers, and new technologies:
elists@oreilly.com

For technical questions about book content:
booktech@oreilly.com

To submit new book proposals to our editors:
proposals@oreilly.com

O'Reilly books are available in multiple DRM-free ebook formats. For more information:
oreilly.com/ebooks

CPSIA information can be obtained at www.ICGtesting.com
Printed in the USA
BVOW10s2030240615

405988BV00014B/105/P